Strata Flor... Talley Abbey

David M. Robinson PhD, FSA

with contributions by Colin Platt PhD, FSA

Introduction

A Monastic Patron: The Lord Rhys

Set in their tranquil green landscapes, the ruined abbeys of St Mary at Strata Florida and St Mary and St John the Baptist at Talley are two of the most captivating medieval monuments to be found in Wales. They were, as we shall see, established for quite different religious orders, following somewhat different monastic codes and with differing customs and precedents for their style of life. But there can be no doubt that the impulse for both foundations stemmed from a single and highly potent source.

With little more than two decades separating their foundation, Strata Florida and Talley were very much a local expression of a movement that had spread like a tidal wave across the whole of western Europe in the late eleventh and early twelfth centuries. This movement, often referred to as the monastic revival, left few corners of the Christian world untouched.

Although the founding fathers of the new religious orders born at this time were driven by an intense spiritual conviction, they could also be inspirational dreamers. Yet dreams alone would not build abbeys of stone. Indeed, success depended in no small measure on the liberal generosity of patrons and benefactors. One such munificent patron in late twelfth-century Wales was Rhys ap Gruffudd (d. 1197), prince of the ancient kingship of Deheubarth. During the reign of King Henry II (1154–89), it was 'Rhys the Great', 'Rhys the Good', who, in a quite staggering reversal of fortunes, restored the political, military, cultural, and spiritual prominence of Deheubarth. And it was Rhys — as an enthusiastic supporter of the new orders — who bound together the early fortunes of Strata Florida and Talley.

Rhys may not have been the true founder of Cistercian Strata Florida in 1164, though he soon assumed the patronage of the fledgling community and certainly merits the title of founder of the abbey's fortunes. Talley, on the other hand, was solely his foundation, established for Premonstratensian canons between 1184 and 1189. Nor did Rhys's monastic patronage stop with these two houses. Possibly as early as the 1160s, he gave his support to Whitland, the mother of the Welsh Cistercian family. Then, about 1180, his was the guiding hand behind the plantation of a community of Cistercian nuns at Llanllŷr (Ceredigion), one of only two such houses for women in Wales. What is more, Rhys's gifts were by no means restricted to the new orders. He is found, for example, offering support to the Norman priory of Benedictine monks at Cardigan, a house located within sight of one of Deheubarth's principal strongholds.

There were marked contrasts between the internal histories of Strata Florida and Talley, and there were even greater contrasts in their degree of architectural splendour. Nevertheless, their foundations were bound together, not only when seen as a reflection of a golden age of monastic revival, but also as a tribute to a remarkably golden era in the Deheubarth of the Lord Rhys.

Opposite: The early fortunes of Cistercian Strata Florida and Premonstratensian Talley were bound together by Rhys ap Gruffudd (d. 1197) — the Lord Rhys — an enthusiastic patron of the new monastic orders in Wales. Rhys was buried in St Davids Cathedral, where this fourteenth-century tomb effigy lies.

In addition to his widespread patronage of the new monastic orders in Wales, the Lord Rhys also supported the foundation of a community of Cistercian nuns at Llanllŷr in Ceredigion. This late thirteenth-century manuscript illustration depicts St Bernard preaching to a group of Cistercian nuns (Copyright Bibliothèque Royale de Belgique, Ms. 1787, f. 8r).

The Welsh Monastic Context

Old and New Monasticism

Monastic life in early twelfth-century Wales was ripe for change. There were still those who recalled the memory of St David, who had, according to his biographer, Rhigyfarch (d. 1099), 'imitated the monks of Egypt, and lived a life like theirs'. However, David's legendary austerities, his hard manual labour, his vegetarian diet, his constant genuflexions and his cold baths were no longer regularly practised by the often self-indulgent hereditary canons of the Welsh *clas* churches. These ancient mother institutions, once the pioneer instruments of Christian conversion, were well-endowed communities, sometimes still headed by hereditary monk-bishops. However, they had learned to guard their spheres of influence too well, and they were riddled with every vice of private property.

Corrupt and archaic though many of the *clasau* may well have become, they were at least Welsh. Unfortunately, it was no help to the earliest reformers of the post-Conquest church that they arrived under the protection of Norman colonizers. Anglo-Norman churchmen never entirely lacked sympathy with the institutions, saints and rituals of the Welsh church. However, what these reformers found was a fossilized institution, badly in need (as they saw it) of life-infusion. And, throughout Wales, they laboured with the insensitive passion of the righteous.

Among the earliest changes were those of the episcopate. There was a Norman bishop of Llandaff by 1107, of St Davids by 1115, of Bangor (following a false start in 1092) from 1120, and St Asaph by 1143. Simultaneously, Norman aristocratic patrons stripped the *clasau* of their wealth, using their endowments for the support of new religious communities. Sheltered by the fortresses of the invaders, these communities were often of superior quality, for Norman monasticism had only recently been reformed itself. Even so, the function of the imported French-speaking monks was always less missionary than supportive. Distrustful of the native Welsh, their first duty was the spiritual care of Norman garrisons. 'Strengthen the locks of your doors', Gilbert Foliot, abbot of Gloucester (1139–48), advised the prior of one of his abbey's cells in distant Wales. It was almost certainly the Benedictine brothers at Ewenny who were urged by Gilbert to surround their house with 'a good ditch and an impregnable wall'.

A colonial reorganization, imposed like this, was almost bound to fail. It was though a failure with more than one cause. During the late eleventh century, the papacy's reform of the western church had barely penetrated Wales. The situation was very different after 1100. The issue at first had been royal control of episcopal appointments. When this was resolved in the formal church-state concordats of the early twelfth century, the reformers turned their attention to the localities. There were two central problems. One was the care of the parish churches, still treated by many landowners as private property. The other was the freedom of monks from their patrons. Dependent priories, established as cells of major abbeys on the Welsh March or in distant France, were no answer to either problem.

Once again, the earliest reformers were Anglo-Normans. Parish churches, it was widely thought, were best entrusted to religious houses — to communities of priests, known as regular canons, who lived according to a rule or code derived from the writings of St Augustine of Hippo (AD 354–430). It was the Augustinians, for this reason, who found greatest favour at the court of King Henry I (1100–35). And, between 1108 and 1118, one of the earliest of these communities in Britain emerged

St David of Wales — who in the late sixth century had 'imitated the monks of Egypt and lived a life like theirs' — from a fifteenth-century manuscript illumination in the Hastings Hours *(British Library, Additional Ms. 54782, f. 40).*

Opposite: The south transept of the twelfth-century Benedictine priory church at Ewenny in the Vale of Glamorgan. The fortress-like architecture of the priory complex seems to echo the advice given to the community by Abbot Gilbert Foliot of Gloucester: 'Strengthen the locks of your doors and surround your house with a good ditch and an impregnable wall'.

Above: Set deep in a glorious valley 'no more than three arrow-shots in width', Llanthony Priory occupied the site of an earlier hermitage. Between 1108 and 1118, the place was given over to one of the leading reformed monastic congregations, the Augustinian canons. Gerald of Wales (d. 1223) thought Llanthony a location 'most suited to the practice of religion'.

Below right: Cîteaux, seen here from the south, was founded as the 'New Monastery' in 1098. It became the head of a vast European monastic order, with thirteen abbeys in Wales (David Robinson).

Opposite: A 'splendid pillar of the church', and abbot of Clairvaux (1115–53), the charismatic St Bernard was without question the most influential figure in the early expansion of the Cistercian order. In this mid-fifteenth-century manuscript illustration by Jean Fouquet, Bernard is depicted preaching to his monks in the chapter house (Musée Condé, Chantilly, Ms. 71, f. 36/Photo RMN, René Gabriel Ojéda).

at Llanthony in the Black Mountains, the patrons of which were exclusively Anglo-Norman. Another Augustinian priory, likewise Anglo-Norman, was established at Carmarthen before 1127; and the much later foundation at Haverfordwest (about 1203–10) was again English rather than Welsh in orientation.

Following closely in the wake of the Augustinian canons, it was soon the turn of the reformed congregations of monks. There were Tironian brothers at St Dogmaels as early as 1113–15, and Savigniac communities were established at Neath in 1130 and Basingwerk in 1131–32 (see map p. 8). Of even greater long-term significance, Cistercian monks arrived at Tintern in the Wye valley in 1131, representing only the second Cistercian foundation in Britain.

All of these new communities featured an eremitical or hermit-like element in their organization, thus emulating the isolated desert existence of the very earliest monastic fathers. They would have agreed with the zealous hermit-monk, Peter Damian, that 'a hermitage is a garden of heavenly delights … [where] the scent of virtues fills the air with fragrance'. Their aim, however, was to live in common, not as anchorites on their own: 'we will follow the rule in all that pertains to the common life so that we will eat, sleep, work and perform the services of God together … [but] we will live as hermits in all that concerns rigorous abstinence and the total renunciation of secular concerns'.

Such common resolve, faithfully performed, gave these men the self-assurance of spiritual storm troops. 'In your land', wrote the Cistercian Bernard of Clairvaux in 1131, addressing King Henry I of England as an equal, 'there is an outpost of my Lord and your Lord … I have proposed to occupy it and I am sending men from my army who will, if it is not displeasing to you, claim it, recover it, and restore it with a strong hand'. 'And this', wrote a thirteenth-century monk-chronicler, 'is what was done'.

The Cistercians and Wales

The Cistercian order, to which Strata Florida belonged, began with the foundation of the 'New Monastery' at Cîteaux (Côte d'Or) in Burgundy in 1098 (see map p. 8). It was here, in a place described by later generations as one 'of horror and of vast solitude', that a group of reformist monks settled to a new life of true austerity and perfect solitude under their leader, Abbot Robert of Molesme (d. 1110). In particular, Robert and his followers were determined to live 'more strictly and perfectly, according to the *Rule* of the most blessed Benedict'. That is they were determined to follow to the letter the monastic code composed by St Benedict of Nursia at Monte Cassino in Italy soon after AD 535.

For at least a decade, the poverty-stricken community at Cîteaux teetered on the brink of destruction. Gradually though the tide began to turn. In the time of Abbot Stephen Harding (1109–33), the number of monks started to multiply, especially after the arrival of the charismatic Bernard of Fontaines (d. 1153) and his companions in 1113. Abbot Stephen, meanwhile, was the man who gave legislative shape to the community's spiritual ideals, providing a solid platform for the expansion and success of the emerging Cistercian order.

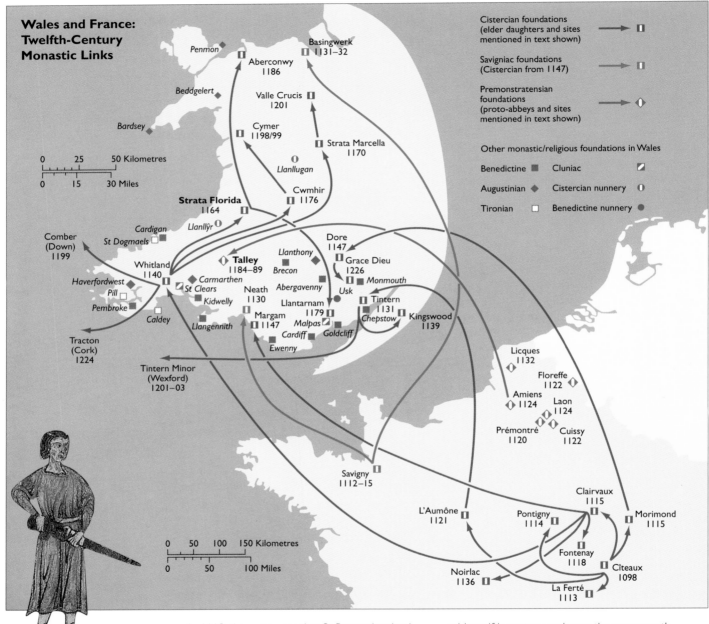

Wales and France: Twelfth-Century Monastic Links

Cistercian foundations (elder daughters and sites mentioned in text shown) →◻

Savigniac foundations (Cistercian from 1147) →◻

Premonstratensian foundations (proto-abbeys and sites mentioned in text shown) →◇

Other monastic/religious foundations in Wales

Benedictine ◼   Cluniac ◿

Augustinian ◆   Cistercian nunnery ◐

Tironian ◻   Benedictine nunnery ●

Penmon
Basingwerk 1131–32
Aberconwy 1186
Beddgelert
Valle Crucis 1201
Bardsey
Cymer 1198/99
Strata Marcella 1170
Llanllugan
0   25   50 Kilometres
0   15   30 Miles
Cwmhir
Strata Florida 1164
Llanllŷr
Cwmhir 1176
Dore 1147
Cardigan
St Dogmaels
Comber (Down) 1199
Llanthony
Grace Dieu 1226
Whitland 1140
Talley 1184–89
Brecon
Monmouth
Haverfordwest
Carmarthen
St Clears
Neath 1130
Abergavenny
Usk
Tintern 1131
Pill
Kidwelly
Llantarnam 1179
Pembroke
Margam 1147
Malpas
Chepstow
Kingswood 1139
Caldey
Llangennith
Cardiff
Goldcliff
Tracton (Cork) 1224
Ewenny
Tintern Minor (Wexford) 1201–03
Licques 1132
Floreffe 1122
Amiens 1124
Laon 1124
Prémontré 1120
Cuissy 1122
0   50   100   150 Kilometres
0   50   100 Miles
Savigny 1112–15
Clairvaux 1115
L'Aumône 1121
Pontigny 1114
Morimond 1115
Fontenay 1118
Noirlac 1136
Cîteaux 1098
La Ferté 1113

The Cistercian abbey of Strata Florida was originally founded by Robert fitz Stephen, Norman lord of Pennardd. This manuscript illustration of Robert dates from the late twelfth century (National Library of Ireland, Ms. 700).

In 1113, the same year that St Bernard arrived, the first daughter colony was sent out from Cîteaux to La Ferté (Saône-et-Loire). Three more 'daughter houses' were established before the end of 1115, including that at Clairvaux (Aube) in Champagne. From the first, this highly celebrated monastery was headed by St Bernard, and from here he became the order's arch-propagandist, taking a major role in the creation of the Cistercian identity. By the

mid-twelfth century, such was the movement's growing success, there were some 350 Cistercian abbeys scattered across most parts of Europe.

In southern Britain, both Waverley and Tintern were settled by monks from L'Aumône (known as 'Petit-Cîteaux'), itself founded in 1121 as a daughter of the great Burgundian mother house. But neither L'Aumône nor Cîteaux ultimately proved influential in the Welsh settlement of the order. The next generation of Cistercian communities to reach Wales were those at Whitland (1140) and Margam (1147). Each took its marching orders from St Bernard of Clairvaux, recruiting directly from his now-flourishing monastery.

As far as potential patrons among the Welsh were concerned, there matters may well have rested. Initial patronage of the budding communities at Whitland and Margam was again decidedly Anglo-Norman. Moreover, Whitland had no real opportunity to send out colonies for several decades, and Margam's plan to found a Welsh daughter house at Pendar (about 1175) in upland Glamorgan appears to have been abandoned before the close of the century.

Eventually, it was once again Norman patronage that allowed Whitland to found a lasting Welsh colony. In June 1164, the abbey was offered a comparatively modest endowment for a daughter foundation in the commote of Pennardd, a district within the Anglo-Norman lordship of Ceredigion. Robert fitz Stephen, the lord of Pennardd, greeted the brothers under their abbot, David, quite possibly on the banks of the Fflur brook. For well over a century, the assumed site has been known as *hen fynachlog* (old monastery). But, within a year of their arrival, circumstances were to change absolutely, not just for this one infant community, but for the whole future of the Cistercians in Wales. The abbey on the Fflur brook — Strata Florida — was to find itself at the mercy of military and political events. As the native chronicle (*Brut y Tywysogyon*) records, 'all the Welsh united to throw off the rule of the French'.

The Norman Clare family had in fact been pushed out of Ceredigion in 1164, and in the following year their vassal, Robert fitz Stephen, was captured. As Anglo-Norman momentum faltered, there emerged a remarkable resurgence in Welsh supremacy in the south-west — the kingdom of Deheubarth. It was Rhys ap Gruffudd (d. 1197), prince of this rich and fertile kingdom, who captured fitz Stephen, and it was Rhys who restored Welsh control to the region. Genial and civilized, long-lived and shrewd, Rhys knew the value of monks in this strategy.

In due course, 'the Lord Rhys', as he is generally known, assumed the patronage of both Whitland and Strata Florida. He especially 'loved and cherished' Strata Florida we are told. If not strictly the founder, he was certainly the effective guarantor of the abbey's fortunes, with his extensive grants confirmed in a

charter of 1184. The ancient *clas* church at Llanbadarn Fawr, some 15 miles (24km) north-west of Strata Florida, and the place where Rhigyfarch had composed his life of St David, was soon eclipsed by the new monastery. Within a decade, Strata Florida was to become the scriptorium where the native Welsh annals were kept. Strengthened by Rhys's generous patronage, the monks made plans to occupy buildings on a more suitable permanent location, where the present ruins now stand. Such was the esteem in which Strata Florida was held by Rhys and his family that it was to become a great tomb-church for the Deheubarth dynasty of princes (p. 55).

Even more significant than Rhys's concern for Strata Florida was his support for the Cistercian order at large. Freed now from the yoke of its Anglo-Norman identity, Whitland was to become the stem of a new tree. A colony of monks left there for Strata Marcella in 1170, and another settled at Cwmhir in 1176. Others went from Strata Florida to Llantarnam in 1179, and to Rhedynog Felen (later moving to Aberconwy) in 1186. In turn, in 1198–99 Cymer was settled from Cwmhir, and in 1201 Valle Crucis was occupied by monks from Strata Marcella. In sum, as we are vividly reminded in the narrative of a thirteenth-century English monk-chronicler, the soldiers of St Bernard's army 'showed forth the discipline of Clairvaux whence they came ... very soon they grew into a great company'.

With the underlying support of the Lord Rhys, Whitland Abbey sent out colonies to Strata Marcella in 1170 and Cwmhir (top) in 1176. In turn, Cymer (above) was colonized from Cwmhir in 1198–99, and the earliest community at Valle Crucis (below) arrived from Strata Marcella in 1201.

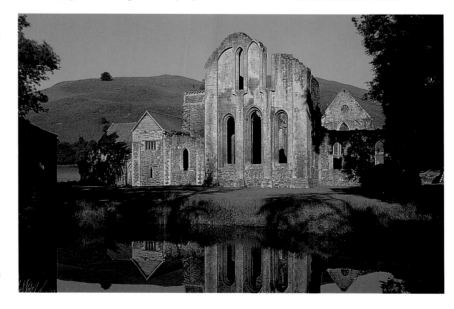

Right: All regular canons (both the Augustinians and Premonstratensians) followed the Rule of St Augustine. *Augustine (d. 430) is shown here in a twelfth-century manuscript from Cîteaux (Bibliothèque Municipale, Dijon, Ms. 638/642, f. 31, Flammarion/ The Bridgeman Art Library).*

Below: A charismatic preacher, Norbert of Xanten (d. 1134) was a close friend of St Bernard of Clairvaux. In 1120 he founded the abbey at Prémontré in north-eastern France — the mother house of the Premonstratensian order. This fresco of St Norbert is in the abbey of SS Severo and Martirio outside Orvieto (Umbria) in Italy, a house refounded for the Premonstratensians in 1226 (© Photo SCALA, Florence, 1990).

The Premonstratensian Canons

St Bernard's Cistercians came to be known as the 'white monks', because of the plain undyed wool of their habits. Unreformed Benedictines were called 'black monks'. The distinction, only of dress in the first instance, inevitably took on other meanings. Before long the regular canons, too, had been divided in the eyes of contemporaries — between white and black, good and bad. This is not to say that the 'black canons', or Augustinians, did not have reformers in their midst, among them the hermit-like brothers of Llanthony (p. 6). But the Augustinian community as a whole was soon over extended; known for its relaxed discipline, sometimes the bad had been welcomed with the good.

Nearest to the Cistercians, in the rigour of their observance, were St Norbert's 'white canons'. A German by birth, Norbert of Xanten (d. 1134) was an instinctive and charismatic preacher. He was in turn hermit, missionary, and archbishop, but most of all he sought the freedom to undertake practical good works. He was a close friend of the Cistercian, Bernard of Clairvaux, sharing his missionary drive. In 1120, Norbert established the mother house of his order at Prémontré (Aisne), in the diocese of Laon. Rather than following the Cistercians in their strict interpretation of the *Rule of St Benedict*, however, Norbert opted for the less formal *Rule of St Augustine* for his community. In particular, its basic practicality may have suited his zeal for the apostolic life. Norbert's white canons soon established a reputation for dedicated prayer, 'pitiable poverty' and 'abundant want': God and man loved them for it.

The subsequent and rapid development of the order owed less to Norbert himself than to Hugh de Fosses (d. 1161), who, in 1128, became the first formally elected abbot of Prémontré. He was a much stronger bureaucrat and organizer than Norbert. It was Hugh who imposed a proper administration for centralized control over a group of monasteries, otherwise only united by respect for Norbert's personal authority. By 1134, statutes had been drawn up that ensured that St Norbert's Premonstratensians would be closely organized on the Cistercian model. In the event, their numerical and geographical expansions were barely less impressive than those of their more celebrated contemporaries. 'In these times', wrote a chronicler in the habit of a white canon, 'the orders of Premonstratensian canons and of Cistercian monks, like two olive-branches in the sight of God, brought to the world the light of piety ... and like fruitful vines, spread the shoots of religion in all directions, and diffusing the fragrance of good repute almost to the limits of the Christian world, founded new abbeys where the worship of God was before unknown'.

The first colony of white canons in England arrived from Licques in the Pays de Calais to settle at Newhouse in Lincolnshire in 1143. By 1160 the initial wave of settlement had produced about fifteen houses. Eventually, there were some thirty-seven abbeys established across Britain. In the heart of Wales (*pura Wallia*), as with the Cistercians, it was Rhys ap Gruffudd who set an example as a patron of the Premonstratensians. The extent to which he embraced the spirit of the reformed orders is perhaps nowhere more clearly illustrated than in his support for his new foundation made at Talley between 1184 and 1189. It was Rhys who, in the late 1180s, ended another chapter in the history of native Welsh monasticism when he bestowed much of the temporal and spiritual income of Llandeilo Fawr — at one time one of the most prestigious *clas* churches of Deheubarth — on the canons who arrived at Talley from their French mother house of St John at Amiens (Somme). In the event, this was to prove the only abbey of the order to be established in medieval Wales. It was to remain a remote outpost in one of the three English circaries (or visitation districts) of Prémontré. Yet in England, at just that time, the order was approaching a new peak in public favour.

That, in part, was the trouble. Prominent among the patrons of the English white canons during this phase was King Henry II's chief justiciar, Ranulf de Glanville (d. 1190), the most powerful royal official in the kingdom. It was Ranulf who founded Leiston Abbey (Suffolk) in 1183, and it was relatives of the chief justiciar who were especially influential in encouraging Premonstratensian expansion. Rhys ap Gruffudd knew Ranulf de Glanville well; they had met in border diplomacy. It was probably Ranulf's good offices on behalf of the white canons that caused Rhys to choose them for Talley. Then, in

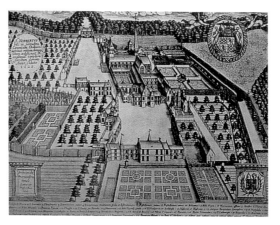

Almost nothing survives of the medieval abbey at Prémontré (Aisne), though this engraving of 1656 shows the church and monastic buildings before their destruction at the time of the French Revolution (Bibliothèque Nationale, Paris).

Premonstratensian Abbeys in Britain

NORTHERN
Dryburgh
French mother house →
Alnwick
Circary boundary - - - -
Holywood
Soulseat
Blanchland
Whithorn   Tongland
Egglestone
Shap   Easby
Coverham
Cockersand   Newhouse
Beauchief   Barlings   Licques
Welbeck   Hagnaby
Tupholme
Dale   Newbo   Wendling
M I D D L E   Croxton
Halesowen   Sulby   West   Langley
Lavendon   Dereham   Leiston
Talley   Beeleigh
S O U T H E R N   Langdon
St John,   Durford   St Radegund's
Amiens   Bayham
Titchfield
Torre   Prémontré

0   50   100 Kilometres
0   30   60 Miles

September 1189, the chief justiciar was dismissed from office. Ranulf's own Leiston canons never got all he had once promised, and Talley's endowment — though reasonable by Welsh standards — proved insufficient to ensure rock-solid foundations. In short, much of the drive had already gone out of the Premonstratensian settlement of Britain, with few houses of any consequence established after this time.

The Premonstratensian abbey at Leiston in Suffolk was founded in 1183 by King Henry II's chief justiciar, Ranulf de Glanville (d. 1190). In the 1360s the canons were obliged to rebuild their house on a fresh site. Extensive remains of the church and monastic buildings survive (English Heritage).

Strata Florida Abbey

The Cistercians of Strata Florida, like many communities of their order, were initially pastoralists. They kept large flocks of sheep and herds of cattle on the adjoining uplands, largely controlled from the farms they called granges. Five or six such upland pastoral farms formed the nucleus of Strata Florida's estates, and these were among the earliest endowments given to the community. Eventually, the number of its granges stood at around fifteen. To these there were annexed further substantial grazing privileges in the surrounding uplands, as well as the revenues of two parish churches: Pencarreg to the south-west, and Llangurig to the north-east. Welsh generosity made the monks rich, but it also brought them a bushelful of problems.

In particular, it was always difficult to persuade princely patrons of the need to preserve Cistercian ideals. Alone in their wilderness at Cîteaux (p. 6), the order's founding fathers had gone hungry rather than accept gifts of manorialized and heavily inhabited land, and had refused to have anything to do with parish churches. Their policy had been strikingly successful. Give them 'a wilderness or forest', wrote Gerald of Wales (d. 1223) of the white monks in the 1180s, 'and in a few years you will find a dignified abbey in the midst of smiling plenty'. But they had brought those wastes under control in the first fury of reform, and with the help of a devout peasant army of lay brethren — the *conversi*. And men of that quality were as hard to find in late twelfth-century Wales as the unencumbered lands they might enclose. From the start, Strata Florida's many granges were less the self-contained farms of the ideal Cistercian model than the hamlets of a still dependent peasantry. Servile tenants (which the first Cistercians had rejected) and appropriated churches (which they abhorred) coexisted in medieval Wales. In the annual debates of the order's General Chapter at Cîteaux, both abuses became a permanent running sore.

This is not to say that any laxity in discipline was not marked for correction. For example, we learn from the order's statutes (*statuta*) that in 1196 there was serious disorder among the lay brothers of Strata Florida. Excessive beer drinking seems to have been at the root of the problem. In any case, the General Chapter ordered the abbot of Whitland to investigate the trouble. This and similar cases led to a total ban on beer at all Welsh granges.

A greater long-term danger for the Strata Florida community was political isolation. The abbey kept its loyalty to its first Welsh patrons, with many of the princes of Deheubarth interred in its buildings. The Lord Rhys's brother, Cadell ap Gruffudd, was buried at the house as early as 1175, and no fewer than nine other princes of the dynasty were laid to rest there (mainly in the chapter house) over the next century. Moreover, Strata Florida's abbots — Deiniol, or Cedifor (in early years), Morgan ap Rhys, or Dafydd ab Owain (in the later Middle Ages) — were as Welsh as the land in which they dwelt. Under such men, it was

Opposite: Strata Florida sits in the pastoral landscape of Ceredigion, at the point where the river Teifi emerges from its upland valley. The abbey is seen here from the south-east. The monks seem to have moved to this site in about 1184, from a temporary mission station a few miles away.

The Cistercians were keen to restore the importance of manual work to the monastic life. Much of the agricultural labour on their estates was undertaken by lay brothers, depicted here in a late twelfth-century manuscript illustration (Bibliothèque Municipale de Troyes, Ms. 392, f. 99v).

Right: In the late thirteenth century, the Strata Florida monks were responsible for compiling the manuscript that forms the basis of Brut y Tywysogyon *(Chronicle of the Princes). This page from* Brut y Tywysogyon *includes a reference to the abbey community entering its new church in 1201 (National Library of Wales, Peniarth Ms. 20, p. 210b).*

Below: Strata Florida's support for the Welsh prince, Llywelyn ab Iorwerth (d. 1240), brought the community into conflict with King John (1199–1216), who in 1212 threatened to destroy the abbey. John was not popular with the Cistercians generally. Indeed, although unsubstantiated, it was said that he was poisoned by a monk of Swineshead Abbey, as portrayed in this late thirteenth-century manuscript illustration (British Library, Cotton Vitellius Ms. A. XIII, f. 5v).

at the abbey that a major history, a lost Latin chronicle, which forms the basis of the *Chronicle of the Princes*, was compiled in the late thirteenth century. It was here, too, that at least one translation of the chronicle into Welsh, *Brut y Tywysogyon*, was composed. In short, the monks of Strata Florida became significant custodians of native cultural traditions.

Yet support for the Welsh cause was also full of risk. Hardly had the monks taken possession of their church (p. 26), celebrating Mass in the choir at Whitsuntide 1201, when their community was in serious jeopardy. As partisans of Llywelyn ab Iorwerth (d. 1240), prince of Gwynedd, they put themselves on the wrong side of King John (1199–1216). No one ever found that a pleasant place to be. In 1212, he issued an order to 'destroy the abbey of Strata Florida, which harbours our enemies ... in so far as you are able'. The king's growing domestic difficulties in the summer of that year caused the abandonment of the Welsh expedition, and may also have been the reason he was prevented from carrying out the threat.

But, despite the disapproval of the English Crown, the Strata Florida community's support for Llywelyn ab Iorwerth continued. Of much greater significance, in October 1238, Llywelyn summoned 'all the princes of Wales' to a great assembly at the abbey. This was a momentous occasion, with a united federation of princes swearing allegiance to Llywelyn's heir, Dafydd (d. 1246). For the age, it was a remarkable symbol of unified statehood. Furthermore, the location chosen for the event speaks volumes of the position the Cistercians now occupied in Welsh public life, not to mention the outstanding importance of Strata Florida itself.

Meanwhile, King John had imposed a heavy fine of £800 on the community, a crippling debt that was still being paid off in 1253. In such circumstances, over-ambitious building programmes would have been difficult to finance, though the greater part of the church and the principal claustral ranges may already have been complete (pp. 28–29). In any case, in 1255 the community purchased its 'great bell', which was presumably placed in the tower over the crossing, and was consecrated by Richard, bishop of Bangor (1236–67). Later in the century, war and misfortune exacted a heavy toll on Strata Florida.

To begin with, King Edward I's Welsh wars of 1276–77 and 1282–83 undoubtedly resulted in some damage to the house. Towards the end of 1284, for example, the community received a payment of £78 by way of compensation for the destruction wreaked during the second war. Very much worse was to come however. According to the chronicler at the Benedictine abbey at Chester, within twelve days of Christmas 1284 the church at Strata Florida was devastated by fire; the Welsh annals place the event in 1286. 'The fire and lightning struck the belfry', wrote the Chester monk, 'and burned the whole of it ... and then devoured the whole church, which was completely covered with lead as far as the walls, except the presbytery'. 'This happened', he tells us, 'in the night'. As if the community had not suffered enough, less than a decade later it was caught up in one of the regional revolts sparked off during the uprising of 1294–95 led by Madog ap Llywelyn, when the abbey was put to the torch by royalist forces. In 1300, however, when granting permission for the abbot and convent 'to construct afresh, and rebuild their house', King Edward proclaimed the action had been 'contrary to our wishes'.

The full extent of the damage at this time is not known. However, various details within the church, perhaps coupled with a rebuilding of the chapter house on a smaller scale (pp. 29–30), suggest shrinkage both in numbers and in wealth. Weakened again by the Black Death in 1348–49, and by subsequent visitations of bubonic plague, the community never fully recovered. In the later medieval centuries, the abbey's lands, for long tended and cultivated by its own lay brothers and servants, were to be leased out in return for cash rents and produce. Indeed, this process had begun with the more distant granges even before 1300. For all this, in the second half of the fourteenth century, Strata Florida may have experienced a period of relative peace, if not prosperity, due largely to the qualities of Abbot Llywelyn Vaughan (1344–80).

As the fifteenth century opened, Strata Florida's resolute Welshness, whilst a prop in many ways, continued to bring it into difficulty. In 1401–02, soon after the outbreak of the Owain Glyn Dŵr rebellion, King Henry IV (1399–1413) took possession of the abbey and temporarily ousted the monks. In the course of the rebellion, English troops were billeted at the house in 1407 and again in 1415. To add to these problems, in 1428 there was a scandalous episode involving John ap Rhys, abbot of the daughter

Above: In the late thirteenth century, it seems certain that Strata Florida suffered some damage during the Welsh wars of King Edward I. In 1300, the king (depicted on this silver penny of his reign) granted the monks permission to rebuild their abbey.

Above left: In 1284/86 Strata Florida was struck by lightning and a subsequent fire swept through the abbey church. Such disasters were not uncommon in the Middle Ages. In this manuscript illustration of about 1190–1200, a monk watches in despair as firefighters seek to douse the flames engulfing his monastery (British Library, Additional Ms. 39943, f. 31v).

house at Aberconwy (by then located at Maenan). Seeking to take Strata Florida as his own, he occupied the abbey 'with a great troop of armed people and archers', disrupting divine service for some forty days. All in all, in 1442 it remained convenient for the monks to lay the entire blame for the sorry state of their house on 'Owain Glyn Dŵr and his company'. So spoiled was the abbey, they claimed, 'the walls of the church excepted … it is not probable that the same can be repaired without the king's aid'.

In spite of all these troubles, there were notable highlights in the fortunes of Strata Florida over the last century of monastic life. Several abbots, especially Rhys (about 1436–41) and Morgan ap Rhys (1444–86), worked hard to raise the spiritual standing of their house, whilst also inaugurating some improvements to the principal buildings. The abbey lived within its means, but at a price. One method of economizing was to accept a cut in the size of the community, reduced to seven monks plus their abbot by the time of the suppression (p. 20). Another, given a complex that now appeared inappropriately large, was to do without repairs to those structures which were presumably no longer in full communal use. Thus, in 1539, when the monks were dispersed, their refectory was reported as ruinous and the infirmary had apparently already collapsed.

A red wax impression of a fifteenth-century seal of Strata Florida Abbey. The Blessed Virgin is seated and crowned, with the cowled figure of the abbot kneeling below and holding a pastoral staff (National Museum of Wales).

Talley Abbey

The Premonstratensian abbey of Talley, in Welsh Talyllychau (literally 'head of the lakes'), takes its name from its situation at the head of two lakes that drain northwards. For Gerald of Wales, Talley was situated 'in a rough and sterile spot, surrounded by woods on every side and beyond measure inaccessible and sufficiently meanly endowed'. Like the Cistercians of Strata Florida, the canons of Talley were again dependent upon the returns of upland granges. But they had another legitimate source of revenue, denied to most Cistercians, in the tithes and further receipts of parish churches and their associated chapelries. On Talley's suppression in 1536, the canons' spiritualities (derived from churches) were of much greater value than their temporalities (the rents from their estates). They had become the custodians of many churches and chapels, including the ancient *clas* at Llandeilo Fawr. It was work to which, in origin, they were especially well suited.

In the late 1180s, when the canons first came to Talley, the possession of private churches was increasingly difficult to defend. Estate churches, doubling for parish use, were still usual in many areas at that date. But virtually all lay landowners who owned parish churches were considering the best method to pass them on. Everywhere there were men who felt no longer morally able to hold on to the possessions of Holy Church. The Premonstratensians clearly offered so much in this respect.

All canons were priests, in theory able to take on parish duties. And while few white canons were actually serving the churches they acquired in England at this time, they were at least able to shoulder the general responsibility for the cure of souls in the parishes. The Premonstratensians, moreover, followed a strict system of government, no less rigorous and demanding than that of the Cistercians. Their order offered other advantages. White canon communities were sometimes smaller and, therefore, potentially cheaper than those of the Cistercians. They could survive from the beginning on the receipts of parish churches, which they could be relied upon to oversee. Rhys ap Gruffudd in the 1180s, contemplating church reform — perhaps even a rekindling of the spirit of the *clas* — may have heard all this recited by Ranulf de Glanville. Both men knew a bargain when they saw one.

Despite the Lord Rhys's generous support, the canons did not establish themselves at Talley without difficulty. Almost immediately, the new community encountered jealousy from its busy and acquisitive Cistercian neighbours, Strata Florida (to the north) and Whitland (to the south-west). Then, between 1193 and 1202, Abbot Peter of Whitland went so far as to attempt to lay claim to Talley, tempting away its canons and seizing its estates, coming close to complete appropriation. And this was only one of the problems encountered by the Premonstratensian brothers over early decades. Rhys had in fact recruited his community not from any English house of the order, but from distant Amiens in north-east France (p. 8). Unappraised of the local situation, the founding canons seem to have commissioned a church that was soon recognized by their successors as far too ambitious. Weakened by the costly quarrel with Whitland, they eventually settled for buildings that were a good deal smaller (pp. 28–29).

Over the next two generations, with support from subsequent Deheubarth princes, the canons added appreciably to their estates. But then, like Strata Florida, they too paid the price for Welsh allegiance. Talley was among the first casualties during King Edward I's conquests in Wales, beginning in 1277.

In the following year it was taken into the king's hands 'by reason of its impoverishment through the Welsh war and by divers inconveniences it has sustained because of that war'. This was the first of

In 1215, an early abbot of Talley, Iorwerth (Gervase), was appointed to the bishopric of St Davids. On his death in 1229, Iorwerth was buried in the cathedral church, where his tomb effigy now lies.

Opposite: The Premonstratensian abbey of Talley (Talyllychau in Welsh) takes its name from its position at the head of two lakes. For Gerald of Wales, it was a 'rough and sterile spot surrounded by woods on every side and beyond measure inaccessible'.

several such unwelcome protections. Accusations of the canons maintaining mistresses suggest discipline at the house was not all that it could be around this time. Between 1278 and 1291, Talley was visited at least four times, with royal assistance, by abbots of English houses of the order. But the underlying fault of the Talley canons was their Welshness. Their patron at the time was Rhys ap Maredudd (d. 1292), who had become a thorn in King Edward's flesh. In a letter sent to the abbot of Prémontré, the king revealed all: his proposal was to expel the canons and to put in their place 'others of the English tongue who are able and willing to observe the religious life'.

In 1285, to underline the king's resolve, the paternal rights over Talley — with powers of visitation and supervision — were granted to Welbeck Abbey in Nottinghamshire (also in the Middle England circary of the order, p. 11). Later these rights passed to the Worcestershire abbey of Halesowen. But Talley stayed far removed, as much in sympathy as location, from the other communities of the entire English province of Prémontré. The distance was one cause of its misrule, but Talley's abbots were not entirely to blame for what went wrong.

After the Black Death, tenants were everywhere in short supply. Wages rose and there were rent riots on many estates. Cash-hungry abbots, unable to find

Landed Estates

For white monk and white canon alike, the acquisition of large tracts of arable land and pasture was essential to the financial prosperity of their abbeys. In this respect, both Strata Florida and Talley benefited chiefly from the generosity of the Deheubarth princes. Initially, where it proved feasible, these lands were exploited by lay brothers from estate centres known as 'granges'.

At its peak, Strata Florida held around fifteen granges. The nucleus of the estates lay in the landlocked uplands around the abbey itself, including the granges of Blaenaeron, Cwmteuddur, Cwmystwyth, Hafodwen, Mefenydd, and Pennardd (the home grange). The last two were in excess of 5,000 acres (2,024ha) each. These core estates provided abundant upland pasture, but the need for land suitable for arable cultivation led to an expansion into other areas, both in river valleys and on the coast. The brothers held the grange of Abermiwl on the Severn, and on the Wye they had another at Aberdihonw. A further string of valuable granges lay on the fringes of Cardigan Bay, including Anhuniog, Morfa Bychan and Morfa Mawr. In all, Strata Florida may have been farming some 6,300 arable acres (2,550ha) at the end of the thirteenth century. The entire estate could have been anything up to five times larger. At the same time,

The Cistercians gained a reputation for clearing extensive areas of woodland to improve their agricultural estates. In this manuscript illustration of about 1111, two Cistercian monks are shown splitting a log (Bibliothèque Municipale, Dijon, Ms. 170, f. 59r).

the monks possessed 1,327 sheep and 428 head of cattle (almost certainly underestimates).

Talley, too, held a large block of upland territory around the abbey site, and exploitation was centred upon the granges of Cefnblaidd, Cilmaharen, Gwastode, Gwyddgrug and Llan y Crwys. To the south were the granges of Carreg Cennen and Ynysdeilo, whereas to the north-west lay Maerdref (bordering the Teifi) and the coastal estate at Aberporth Blaenannerch. Further afield, near Abergavenny, Talley held lands, which were the gift of William de Braose (d. 1211), an Anglo-Norman patron. William's daughter had married the eldest son of Talley's founder, the Lord Rhys. In the uplands of the lordship of Gower, the canons also held property granted by John de Braose (d. 1232).

According to the ideals of their orders, the abbots of Talley and Strata Florida would have aimed to establish balanced and thriving mixed agricultural economies on their granges and other landed estates. To this end, at first they were guided by the preference for direct exploitation, employing the services of a willing lay brotherhood. Nevertheless, there are clear indications of a certain duality from a very early period (p. 13), with tenants — obliged to render certain dues — present across the holdings of both abbeys. By the late thirteenth century, financial difficulties (common to the monasteries of south Wales), coupled with broader economic trends, led to a wholesale move towards such duality. Monasteries began to lease out more and more of their estates in return for regular fixed the money elsewhere, resorted to the expedient of selling pensions. In the early 1380s, at the petition of Abbot Rhys, Talley was once more in the king's hands. It was said to be 'injured by oppression', with the negligence of previous abbots cited for its impoverishment 'by corrodies [pensions] and debts and the withholding of rents'. The abbey's sufferings were not yet over, since, like the monks at Strata Florida, the Talley canons were caught up in the turmoil of the Owain Glyn Dŵr rebellion. Some years after, in 1427, at least one of the canons (Mathew ap Llywelyn Ddu) was still being hunted for treason. A few years later, in May 1430, it was Abbot Dafydd who sought royal protection for his house for

the third time, claiming it was 'wasted by misrule and vexatious lawsuits'.

Isolation continued to prove a weakness. Talley was the only white canon community to which the energetic improver, Bishop Richard Redman (d. 1505), one-time abbot of Shap, never came during all his forty years as reforming commissary-general of the English province of Prémontré. Even in Wales, where few monastic superiors of the late Middle Ages went uncelebrated in song, Talley's abbots rated scarcely a mention. The demise of the abbey in 1536 was equally silent.

This fifteenth-century brass seal matrix belonged to Talley Abbey. At the top is the Agnus Dei (Lamb of God) symbol, with a mitred abbot below. The connection is obscure, but the matrix was found at Wymondham in Norfolk (Norwich Castle Museum, Norfolk Museums Service).

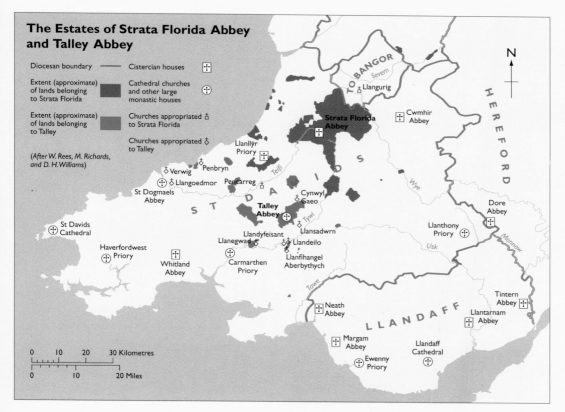

The Estates of Strata Florida Abbey and Talley Abbey

Diocesan boundary

Extent (approximate) of lands belonging to Strata Florida

Extent (approximate) of lands belonging to Talley

(After W. Rees, M. Richards, and D. H. Williams)

Cistercian houses ⊞

Cathedral churches and other large monastic houses ⊕

Churches appropriated to Strata Florida

Churches appropriated to Talley

Sheep farming was important to the economy of each of the two abbeys. To varying degrees, and with changes over time, their upland flocks were tended by both lay brothers and tenants. This fourteenth-century manuscript illustration shows a man and woman tending sheep in a small pen (British Library, Additional Ms. 42130, f. 163v).

cash rents. There are signs that Talley had already begun to make such moves long before 1300, and by the mid-fourteenth century Strata Florida was in much the same position.

By the time of the suppression in the 1530s the transformation was virtually complete, with

very little remaining in the direct control of the abbeys. Most of Talley's lands were administered by a lay steward. As well as rents, Strata Florida received much in the way of 'customary' payments from its estate tenants, including oats, corn, capons, eggs and sheep.

A manuscript illumination of King Henry VIII (1509–47) from the opening folio of the Valor Ecclesiasticus *of 1535 (National Archives, PRO, E 344/22).*

The Suppression and After

The economic and political crises of the fourteenth and fifteenth centuries had taken their toll on the monastic houses of Wales. Financial poverty had been a problem for many throughout the later Middle Ages, and by the early 1500s the days of innovative farming and astute estate management were long since over. The numerical strength of communities had been consistently weakened from the mid-fourteenth century, and there had been occasional disruptions to the daily round of prayer and worship. Even before the accession of King Henry VIII to the English throne in 1509, wherever we look — in recruitment, in patronage, in general support — the ideals of the cloister had largely lost their appeal. The spiritual drive that had fuelled the fires of the monastic revival four hundred years before had been exhausted.

Incidents of scandal, which occasionally there were, could only make things worse. In 1534, for instance, a charge of counterfeiting coins levelled against a monk at Strata Florida shows, if nothing else, a serious lack of discipline at the house. A year later, as rumours spread across the country, there was little the Welsh monasteries could do to withstand the impending suppression. Moreover, few people, gentry or otherwise, were prepared to resist on their behalf. Almost everywhere the situation was very much the reverse, with men queuing up to take advantage of the opportunities offered by the looming change.

Before any definite move, King Henry needed a comprehensive report and valuation of property held by the monasteries throughout the kingdom. Known as the *Valor Ecclesiasticus*, the document was compiled in 1535. It gave a fairly clear picture of the houses in Wales, none of which had an income in excess of £200. On the face of it, Strata Florida at £118 and Talley at £136 were houses of moderate rank, but £200 was the figure set as the benchmark for continuance by the king. In March 1536 an Act was passed whereby all monasteries whose possessions could not yield this annual figure were to be given up (suppressed), 'forasmuch as manifest sin, vicious, carnal, and abominable living is daily used and committed among the little and small abbeys, priories and other religious houses of monks, canons and nuns, where the congregation of such religious persons is under the number of twelve persons'. The news must have appeared especially bleak to the eight monks at Strata Florida, as it would to the eight canons then resident at Talley.

Talley's end came in that year, though Strata Florida was initially spared. The abbey made a last-ditch effort, struggling to raise the necessary finance, and buying its survival for the sum of £66. Its reprieve was to last less than three years, and in February 1539 Strata Florida, too, was closed. Abbot Richard Talley (1516–39) and his seven remaining monks all received pensions.

Following the suppression, the outlying properties of Premonstratensian Talley were variously disposed of, but a sizeable portion of the estates in close proximity to the abbey was retained by the king, and was to form the Crown manor of Talley. The abbey church was spared from immediate destruction (p. 31), and until 1772 it was to serve the needs of the parish.

At Strata Florida, Sir Richard Devereux (d. 1547) was appointed receiver-general of the abbey's lands and his father, Lord Ferrers (d. 1559), was made steward. Shortly before he died, Devereux secured a lease on the estates and the greater part of these passed to his heirs, the earls of Essex. By 1567, the site of the abbey itself had been acquired by John Stedman (d. 1613), and in the late seventeenth century it was perhaps Richard Stedman (d. 1702/03) who built or rebuilt the house, Great Abbey Farm, which still stands over parts of the former claustral buildings. In 1744, Richard Stedman junior died without heir, and the house (with the ruins of the abbey church) were to pass to his brother-in-law, Thomas Powell (d. 1752) of Nanteos.

The Valor Ecclesiasticus *gave Henry VIII a comprehensive valuation of every religious house in England and Wales. This is the folio giving the assessment of Strata Florida Abbey. The net annual income of the house (Et sic reman' clare) is given as £118 7s. 3d. This was below the benchmark set by the king in 1536 for the continuance of monastic life (National Archives, PRO, E 344/22, f. 130v).*

Ystrad Flur (Strata Florida) the Ruins and modern chapel with the Teivi

Both Talley and Strata Florida attracted the attention of the energetic Stephen Williams (1837–99), a Victorian railway engineer and something of a pioneer in the field of monastic archaeology. Although archaeological interest in Strata Florida was first stimulated in 1847, it was the work by Williams in 1887–90 which was to recover many details of the medieval buildings for the modern age. His work at Talley, in 1892–94, was less extensive and less spectacular in terms of results. Nevertheless, the importance of both sites to the Welsh nation was clearly demonstrated.

By the 1930s Strata Florida and Talley lay in the hands of the Representative Body of the Church in Wales. It was that body which entrusted the guardianship of the ruins (Strata Florida in 1931 and Talley in 1933) to the commissioners of HM Office of Works. Programmes of clearance, excavation and conservation began soon afterwards. Today responsibility for the care of both abbeys rests with Cadw, the historic environment service of the Welsh Assembly Government.

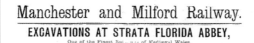

Above: From the late eighteenth century, the ruins of Strata Florida and Talley began to attract the interest of both antiquarians and artists in search of the Picturesque. This watercolour of Strata Florida from the north-west was executed around 1840–50 by the Revd John Parker (National Library of Wales).

In the late 1880s, cheap excursions to see the excavations at Strata Florida ('One of the Finest Buildings of Mediæval Wales') were advertised by the Manchester and Milford Railway.

Building the Abbeys

In Search of Style

Both Strata Florida and Talley belonged to very large European monastic families, each with a strength of kinship which transcended national boundaries in a way that is difficult to comprehend more than eight centuries later. These European ties were true not only in terms of the constitutional frameworks of the two orders; in part at least, and for much of the twelfth century, the same might be said of the style and layout to be found in the architecture of Cistercian and Premonstratensian abbey churches and monastic buildings.

Although much of the upstanding fabric at these two houses has long since disappeared, the ground plans of their churches were first uncovered in excavations at the end of the nineteenth century. In addition, we can trace a little more of their original detail from antiquarian accounts, prints and early photographs. Moreover, for Strata Florida in particular, the abundance of architectural stone fragments recovered from the site can provide invaluable clues in trying to understand the various features of the medieval superstructure.

Looking at other important ecclesiastical buildings raised across south Wales in the late twelfth and early thirteenth centuries — notably the cathedrals of St Davids and Llandaff — there can be no doubt of the involvement of English-trained masons in their design. Indeed, the same can be said of many significant architectural works in Ireland during the same era. In other words, then, it would not be surprising were we to encounter a balance of architectural characteristics at both Strata Florida and Talley. On the one hand, we might expect to see a reflection of the austere simplicity seen in the earliest Cistercian and Premonstratensian buildings in the cradle-lands

of the orders. And, on the other, we are very likely to find evidence of the marked regional style, itself transmitted by itinerant masons who were probably recruited from the larger architectural lodges in the west of England.

A Temporary Site

About 1.5 miles (2.4km) to the south-west of Strata Florida there is a site still known as *hen fynachlog*, 'old monastery' (now a private farm). For well over a century there has been a strong tradition that this was the site where, in the summer of 1164, a colony of monks arrived from Whitland Abbey to establish a daughter house (p. 9). Before the settling community arrived, it would have been normal Cistercian practice for the patron to have erected timber buildings to serve as temporary accommodation. Following negotiations with Whitland, Robert fitz Stephen probably made such provision near the waters of the Fflur brook.

The military success of the Lord Rhys in 1165 may have had little immediate effect on the young colony's building programme, and there are indications that stone construction was soon in hand. Today, in what seems a rather restricted site, there is little evidence of definite structures beneath the turf. Nevertheless, from hearsay evidence recorded in the nineteenth century, there is the possibility that the foundations of a modest abbey church, measuring some 126 feet by 42 feet (38.4m by 12.8m), still remain for closer investigation. Such proportions would not be out of step with those suggested for two of the earliest British Cistercian churches, Tintern and Waverley. It seems, too, that churches of modest size continued to be a feature of the order through the twelfth century, especially where the scale of monastic recruitment and economic stability had yet to be confirmed.

This capital from the south transept at Strata Florida is one of the many beautifully carved pieces of stonework recovered during the excavations of 1887–90. The masons appear to have learnt their trade under the influence of workshops in the west of England.

A strong tradition places the site of hen fynachlog *(old monastery) on the banks of the Fflur brook. The foundations of an early Cistercian stone church may lie somewhere beneath the turf.*

Opposite: Ultimately, the inspiration for the Cistercian architectural aesthetic, which appeared across England and Wales in the mid- to late twelfth century, was derived from the order's cradle-lands in Burgundy and Champagne. Fontenay Abbey (Côte-d'Or), for example, was a daughter of St Bernard's Clairvaux. Its austere but beautiful twelfth-century church has often been taken to represent the very embodiment of early Cistercian architectural practice (David Robinson).

New Sites: French Links

In 1184 the Lord Rhys granted a charter of endowments to the community at Strata Florida, and between 1184 and 1189 he brought the Premonstratensian canons to Talley. These two events mark the next stage in the history of the buildings.

In his charter to the Cistercian house, Rhys proclaimed to everyone that he had 'begun to build the venerable monastery called Strata Florida, and after building it have loved and cherished it'. If not before, this surely indicates that the plans to move to a new location had by then been finalized, and arrangements for the earliest stone buildings on the present site were well in hand. Meanwhile, the Premonstratensians who arrived from north-east France found a suitable location at Talley from the outset. Initially, like their spiritual neighbours, the Talley canons almost certainly served God in timber buildings, but they too were just as ambitious to lay foundations for an imposing stone church.

Taken from a triptych of 1450, this painting shows Cistercian monks building the twelfth-century abbey church at Maulbronn in Germany. It is a romanticized scene, since in reality the white monks are unlikely to have taken the lead in their church building programmes. Lay brothers may have been involved, but most of the work was done by experienced secular masons (Landesmedienzentrum Baden-Württemberg).

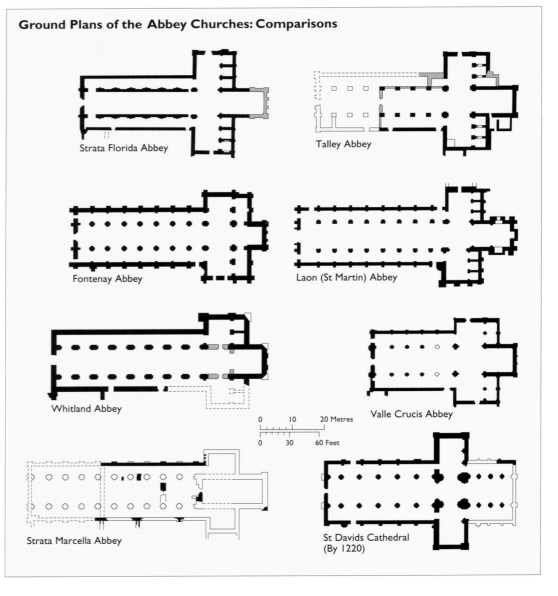

Ground Plans of the Abbey Churches: Comparisons

Strata Florida Abbey

Talley Abbey

Fontenay Abbey

Laon (St Martin) Abbey

Whitland Abbey

Valle Crucis Abbey

0   10   20 Metres

0   30   60 Feet

Strata Marcella Abbey

St Davids Cathedral
(By 1220)

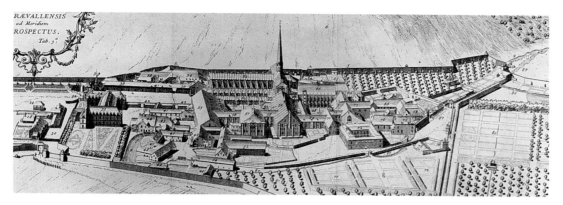

RÆVALLENSIS
ad Meridiem
ROSPECTUS.
Tab. 3ª.

Clairvaux Abbey seen from the south in an engraving of 1708, before the destruction of the church. It was the new church built at Clairvaux during the lifetime of St Bernard (probably about 1135–45) which provided the model for other houses in the family to follow, including those in Wales (Bibliothèque Nationale, Paris).

A comparison of the ground plans of the two abbeys as devised demonstrates a marked similarity in scale and basic planning. At Strata Florida, in particular, the square east end, the layout of the presbytery and transepts, their proportions and overall mass were all ultimately derived from the Burgundian heartlands of the Cistercian order. The resulting ground plan is widely known as 'Bernardine', after St Bernard of Clairvaux. Thought to have been based on a set of proportional principles, the 'Bernardine' plan was at its most popular during the second half of the twelfth century, and is to be found at numerous Cistercian sites across Europe. Similarly, the inspiration for the Talley plan must have been French in origin; and, in turn, Premonstratensian architecture in north-east France was heavily influenced by Cistercian precedents. But the ground plans alone, if ultimately of French inspiration, cannot reveal all.

As we have seen (p. 9), the initial community sent out to Strata Florida in 1164 came from Whitland, itself established as a daughter of St Bernard's Clairvaux. And it was probably the functional austerity of the now-lost church — known to have been raised at this celebrated house about 1135–45 — that provided the model not only for Whitland, but also for contemporary Margam. One very significant aspect of the initial ground plan at Whitland is the absence of any substantial support for a central tower. In fact, broadly speaking, the completed church is very likely to have resembled others in the Clairvaux family built during St Bernard's lifetime, with that at Fontenay Abbey (Côte-d'Or) frequently cited as the embodiment of the form. Founded in 1118, the church at this very well known Burgundian house has traditionally been dated to about 1139–47. At the east end, the presbytery and transepts were roofed at a lower level than the

Left: The design of the church at Fontenay in Burgundy is based on the classic 'Bernardine' plan. As this view of the east end shows, Fontenay lacked a central tower, and the presbytery was set at a lower level than the nave. The traditional dating of the building (1139–47) has become controversial, and it may have taken on its final form marginally later in the twelfth century (The Art Archive/Dagli Orti).

Left: The east end of the church at Noirlac (Cher) was also based on the so-called Fontenay model, without a regular crossing or central tower, although here the transepts were roofed at the same level as the nave. The original scheme for Strata Florida may have been similar in style (Hervé Champollion/akg-images).

nave, a feature that eliminated any form of regular crossing and central tower. This arrangement was by no means uncommon in France in the mid-twelfth century, though there were variations in the basic form. At Noirlac (Cher), for instance (a building of the 1150s), although the transepts were roofed at the same level as the nave, the presbytery was distinctly lower.

All in all, it seems the designs of Whitland and Margam almost certainly mirrored the 'Bernardine' pattern, and the same might be said of the mid-twelfth-century churches constructed at Rievaulx in the north of England and Melrose in Scotland. This distinctive characteristic also featured in a number of Irish Cistercian churches built before 1200, including Baltinglass and Boyle.

A cutaway drawing to show the east end of the abbey church at Strata Florida as it may have been first designed. The presbytery is reconstructed in the Fontenay style, with a roof lower than that of the transepts and the proposed nave. The scheme was to be modified, probably as work on the nave progressed (Illustration by Terry Ball, 1998).

The Late Twelfth Century

At Strata Florida, although the evidence is complex, on balance it seems very likely that the east end of the 'Bernardine' church begun in the time of the Lord Rhys featured a superstructure akin to the Fontenay model. And, from the upstanding remains, together with the many loose stonework fragments recovered in the excavations of 1887–90, we are able to trace variations in the stylistic detail of the emerging abbey church.

As with the contemporary rebuilding of St Davids Cathedral, ornamental variety was often encouraged

in twelfth-century architectural planning, and it cannot be considered a foolproof guide to chronology. Nevertheless, at the east end of Strata Florida there are sufficient indications to suggest that the construction programme began with the south transept and its three rib-vaulted chapels, gradually moving towards the crossing piers and the north transept, and also taking in the initially short, low presbytery. Assigning precise dates to this work is difficult, though it would not be unreasonable to suggest that Rhys's charter of 1184 actually marked the completion of a significant stage in building.

Thereafter, although the church was unfinished when Rhys died in 1197, a key date is recorded in *Brut y Tywysogyon* (*Chronicle of the Princes*) just four years later. In 1201, the chronicler noted, 'the community of Strata Florida went to the new church on the eve of Whit Sunday, after it had been nobly and handsomely built'.

By this stage, whether a true Fontenay-style arrangement at the east end had been fully completed or not, the scheme had quite definitely been modified. Again we have a few clues that suggest the course of events. In particular, it is clear that the presbytery was extended eastwards and a stone rib vault was inserted. Also, details of the western arch, which stood over one side of the central crossing, suggest that it is a secondary feature, not least because one of the corbels on which the arch rested was reused from elsewhere. Together, the evidence suggests a deliberate transition to a formalized crossing, with plans for a squat tower or belfry above.

The work on the greater part of the nave and the west front had followed, and, from what we know of the completed church, there is much evidence for involvement by the regional school of masons. Distinct similarities between the arcade piers here at Strata Florida and those in the nave at St Davids Cathedral can, for example, be paralleled elsewhere in the West Country. The details of the beautifully carved capitals that stood on top of the Strata Florida piers tell us they could only have been derived from the same workshop as several examples at St Davids, if not — in some instances — the same hand. In turn, the very same general body of masons can be identified working at Strata Florida's sister church at Strata Marcella and also at Valle Crucis. It is also interesting to note that at

Strata Marcella (founded in 1170) a case could again be argued for a Fontenay-style arrangement at the east end, though at Valle Crucis (founded in 1201) the formal crossing and tower were planned at the outset (see plans p. 24).

In the meantime, events at Talley had reached something of a hiatus. At first, although it was Strata Florida he 'loved and cherished', the Lord Rhys must also have shared in the considerable ambitions of his Talley community. One of the canons who had arrived here from Amiens in distant France had probably been chosen for his practical bent, as well as for his experience of the architectural aspirations of the order. Encouraged by the founder's benefactions, the original scheme for the scale of the church matched that devised for Strata Florida. Like the nearby Cistercian house, its monumental proportions would have rivalled those of the cathedral at St Davids. The loss of St John at Amiens means we cannot say whether it served as the model for Talley, but the proposed church certainly approached the scale of that at the important Premonstratensian house of St Martin at Laon (Aisne). Indeed, despite the extreme austerity of its superstructure, Talley would have far outstripped the size of those twelfth-century churches of the order in England, particularly since most were planned with aisleless naves. Moreover, although the white canons apparently shared the early Cistercian indifference for crossing towers, Talley seems to have been planned with a stone tower from the outset.

As at Strata Florida, building began at the east end of the church, with the presbytery, the crossing and the transepts — each with three barrel-vaulted eastern chapels. From the earliest progress, however, it is clear that the architectural detail lacked the quality and richness of its Cistercian cousin. The foundations of the nave, including the piers of the proposed aisle arcades, were laid out without significant interruption. It was at this point, shortly after 1193, that Abbot Peter of Whitland made a desperate bid to convert the abbey into a white monk house (p. 17), and Talley became embroiled in a struggle for its very survival as a Premonstratensian community. A costly litigation quarrel ensued. It was not until the early years of the thirteenth century that the successful, but greatly impoverished, canons returned to their unfinished abbey church and monastic buildings.

Above: Much of the architectural detailing in the abbey church at Strata Florida bears close comparison with St Davids Cathedral. In particular, ornamental variety was a feature of both buildings. The nave at St Davids, seen here from the west end, was begun in the 1180s.

Had the Talley canons been able to complete their church to the original plan, its scale would have approached that of the important Premonstratensian abbey of St Martin, Laon (Aisne) in north-east France (David Robinson).

A Tour of Talley Abbey

Layout of the Abbey

Talley Abbey is set in a pastoral landscape of undulating hills on a watershed between two streams, one of which flows northwards from the Talley lakes towards the river Cothi. The other stream, running off Mynydd Cynros above the site, must have provided the abbey's water supply and drains south into the Dulais, joining the Tywi near Llandeilo. From the main road skirting the lakes and the ruins, the remains of the tower stand out as the most prominent feature. The minor road, which leads into the village, brings you to the west side of the abbey.

A modern gate and wooden steps provide access, and ahead are the low foundations of the church, with a view eastwards towards the tower and presbytery. To the right (south) are the slight remains of the cloister, around which the monastic buildings were grouped. Modern structures outside the current boundary lie over other monastic remains.

The Abbey Church

Had the abbey church been raised to its original plan, it would have been some 240 feet (73m) long, with a nave of eight bays, representing one of the largest Premonstratensian churches in Britain. At the bottom of the steps into the site, you will see the low stone footings of walls to the right, and the stubs of three pairs of arcade piers ahead. These features mark those parts of the building begun in the late twelfth

A short flight of wooden steps leads down from the car park to the abbey ruins. From here, there is a mixture of level gravelled paths and grass.

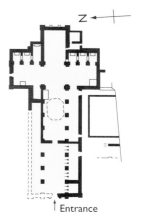

↑ Entrance

Left: A drawing illustrating three aspects of the church at Talley: the surviving ruins appear in solid detail; the cutaway reconstruction suggests the form of the completed building; and the ambitious scale of the initial scheme is depicted in outline (Illustration by Terry Ball, 1998).

Opposite: A general view of the abbey church at Talley looking eastwards towards the remains of the crossing tower and the presbytery. The monastic buildings lay around the cloister to the (south) right.

Above: The west doorway into the completed nave at Talley seems to have been comparatively narrow. There is no surviving decoration.

A view eastwards along the proposed north aisle of the nave at Talley. The original plan was abandoned after one bay, with blocking walls inserted between the nave piers (right).

Almost all of the rubble piers in the nave at Talley were devoid of architectural ornament. The one exception was the eastern pier on the south side, which stood on a chamfered plinth and had simple moulded corners. The pier shows signs of collapse or subsidence.

century, but apparently abandoned soon afterwards. Today, the area is grass covered so as to distinguish it from the canons' church as it was eventually completed in the early thirteenth century.

Just at the bottom of the modern wooden steps, the threshold and the right-hand side of the proposed west doorway survive. The pier stubs, of plain rubble construction, stand up to 3 feet (0.9m) high. Excavations failed to reveal any trace of foundations for a northern wall at this end of the church. It has been suggested, however, that plans were made for towers at the west end of the original nave. Indeed, a thick wall runs between the first of the southern piers and the outer line of the church. But this wall is not bonded into the adjacent masonry at either end, and it seems unlikely that it would have supported a structure of any great height.

You will see that the turf covering in the unfinished south aisle is slightly higher than in the remainder of the nave. There is no obvious reason for this, and had the building programme been completed to plan this would probably have been levelled. In this same unfinished aisle, further to the east, there is the site of a doorway, robbed of its dressed stone jambs. In the initial plan, the door may have been intended to give the canons access to the west walk of a large cloister court.

The Nave

The nave, as eventually completed, can now be identified by the gravel floor covering. It stands beyond the cross wall, which represents the west front of the completed abbey church. From the plan (inside back cover), it is clear that the north aisle was virtually abandoned, with blocking walls inserted between the piers. The nave thus comprised four central bays (a bay is defined as the space between each pier), along with the corresponding length of the south aisle.

The west doorway into the nave is comparatively narrow and has no surviving decoration. The door was also used after the suppression, when the church served the parish, though the threshold was then set at a higher level. Inside, very little survives to create any impression of the original appearance of the monastic church. The rectangular piers were largely built of coarse rubble, though you will see that the easternmost example on the south side stood on a chamfered plinth and had moulded corners. Moreover, we should remember this is not the entire medieval picture. Discoveries from the excavations of the 1890s suggest that the walls were plastered and decorated in colour, and at least some of the windows were filled with painted glass. Parts of the floor, too, were covered with decorated tile pavements.

Two doorways led from the south aisle into the cloister alleys, or walkways, outside. The surviving remains of the east doorway preserve original detailing, whereas the doorway to the west was modified after the suppression.

Lay brothers, so important during the early years of the Cistercians, were never such a great force within the Premonstratensian order. The space required for them within the nave at Strata Florida (pp. 40–43), for example, was not repeated here at Talley. Instead, from no late stage in the Middle Ages, the nave at Talley is likely to have served the community within the vicinity of the abbey. Surrounding tenants in the valleys and hills would have gathered to worship at a parochial altar set up against a stone or wooden screen dividing the nave of the church from the canons' choir beyond.

Old photographs show the Drummond mausoleum (now marked out in the gravel) raised over the ruins of the medieval nave, and the square block of masonry, which remains set against the northern wall, marks a somewhat older tomb of the family.

The Canons' Choir and the Crossing Tower

The daily life of the community was focused upon the *opus Dei* (the work of God). From very early morning, and through the day, the canons gathered in the choir to recite and sing their principal services, composed of psalms, prayer, the Scriptures, and Masses. Each canon took his place in wooden choir stalls, arranged on three sides of the central crossing, with a clear view east towards the high altar. The tower was situated above this area.

Only the eastern and northern arches of the crossing remain standing, with two walls of the tower rising above. The north-east pier, which links the two surviving arches, has moulded shafts at its angles, though even this simple decoration stops where the arches begin to spring outwards. As suggested (p. 28), this probably reflects the poverty in which the community found itself on its return to Talley following the Whitland dispute of the 1190s.

The walls of the tower now stand to a maximum height of approximately 85 feet (26m), though a photograph of about 1875 shows a corbelled-out

This early photograph of Talley, taken about 1875, shows the crossing tower from the north-east. The corbelled-out upper stage fell in 1895, apparently after a severe frost.

Below: The moulded shafts on the angles of the north-east crossing pier at Talley stop at the point where the arches begin to spring outwards. This change of form probably reflects the community's relative poverty in the early thirteenth century.

upper stage indicating an original height in excess of 95 feet (29m). Narrow staircases run in passages within the thickness of the walls, and these follow the line of the pointed arches. You will best see the scale of the passages from the opening on the nave side of the northern arch. From this same point, notice the two openings in the eastern wall of the tower. The lower one is square headed, and directly above this is a slightly pointed window. A row of beam holes can be seen running below the base of the pointed window, marking the position of a wooden ceiling.

The stump of the south-west crossing pier shows signs of collapse or subsidence, as does the nearest pier in the nave. This may explain why the tower was early ruined on two sides.

The Presbytery

At the east end, the presbytery was the liturgical focus of the canons' church and the site of the high altar. After the suppression it was used as the chancel of the parish church. Later still, part of the eastern crossing arch was blocked and a smaller chancel built within the medieval presbytery.

*The abbey church at Talley was
begun in the late twelfth century
and completed, in modified form,
in the early thirteenth century.
This cutaway reconstruction
provides an impression of the
internal arrangements. Of
necessity, the window details,
the position of the choir stalls,
and the form of the roofs over
the transept chapels are all
conjectural interpretations
(Illustration by Terry Ball, 1998).*

Although all such later works were removed when
Talley was taken into State care, few of the original
features survived. There were no signs of an altar,
or of any floor tiles. But discoveries during the
excavations of the 1890s suggest that the eastern
wall was pierced by three lancet windows set
between buttresses on the outer face. The scale
of the east wall, with its massive corner buttressing,
suggests that a stone vault was at least planned if not
actually completed.

Traces of a plain recess set into the southern wall
may indicate a sedilia, or a group of three seats used
by the canons officiating during a Mass. To the right,
there are two doorways in this same south wall.
That nearest the crossing communicated with the

northernmost chapel of the south transept. The
second doorway gave access to a small room that
could also be entered from outside the church.
From this room, another doorway led into a chamber
that probably served as the sacristy. It was here that
the vestments and sacred vessels used in the church
were stored under the care of one of the canons
who served as the sacrist.

The Transepts

To the north and south of the crossing, the transepts
formed the cross arms of the church. On the east side
of each transept, a simple arcade raised on square
piers led into three diminutive chapels. These chapels
provided altars for the priest-canons to celebrate their
daily private Mass. Masses were also said for the souls
of the dead, and particularly for the souls of important
patrons and benefactors. Rhys ap Maredudd (d. 1292),
for example, a descendant of the Lord Rhys, was a
patron of the house and was granted the special
privilege of the confraternity of the Premonstratensian
order. He was thus regularly commemorated with
particular honour at one of the Talley altars.

In the north transept, the doorway in the
northern wall may have given access to the canons'
cemetery, probably situated to the east of the church.
Just east of this doorway, a stair was contained within
the thickness of the wall, leading up to the roof space
above the chapels. The rectangular stone plinth
against the west wall appears to be medieval, but we
cannot be certain of its purpose; perhaps it was the
base of a tomb. The archway to the left (south) of
this plinth was the only means of entering that small
section of the north aisle which seems to have been
completed. The line of the roof crease over the
single bay can be seen on the nave side.

The three eastern chapels in the north transept
were designed to be covered with pointed barrel
vaults, a distinct characteristic that may have been
borrowed from Burgundian Cistercian models.
Against the presbytery wall, there are traces of the
vault that covered the west side of the southernmost
chapel. Stone bases representing the altars in all
three chapels survive, and plain brownish floor tiles
of an apparently late medieval type can be seen in
several places. The walls between each chapel were
originally intended to be solid, though they were
apparently pierced as open arches in a modification
of the earlier thirteenth century.

The southern chapel was further modified with an eastwards extension. Although it is assumed this work was again carried out in the first half of the thirteenth century, it cannot be confirmed. There is a staircase in the extended north wall, with indications that the jambs in the opening were reused. You will see the base of the east window, and below this the altar plinth with wing walls to either side. In the south wall, within an arched recess, there is a piscina (a small sink in which the sacred vessels were cleansed). The extension of the chapel meant this was left in a position unusually far from the altar.

On the opposite side of the crossing, the arrangements in the south transept were broadly similar. In the south-west corner, however, you will see a stone plinth, which perhaps represents the base of a staircase. This would be perfectly normal in a monastic church, since it was the usual position of the night stairs. The dormitory was probably situated on the first floor of a range of buildings running south from this transept. The canons would have entered the church for services at night via such stairs.

Turning to face the eastern chapels, high above the slight traces of the arch leading into the northernmost example, you will see the left-hand splay of a small clerestory window. Traces of the barrel vault for this chapel again survive very clearly against the presbytery wall. The altar bases in all three chapels survive, but the floor tiles had all been robbed out before the end of the nineteenth century. Between the chapels, there is good evidence of the way the original partition walls were broken and finished with flat faces during the modifications of the thirteenth century.

The Cloister and Monastic Buildings

The two doorways (p. 35) in the south aisle of the nave led out into the cloister court. Essentially, this was a central open square — probably serving as a garden — and typically it would have been surrounded on its four sides by covered passageways known as alleys. Today, the only traces to survive are the low walls that supported open arcades facing on to the court. The monastic buildings were normally

arranged around three sides of the cloister, with the church closing off the fourth side.

In terms of the east range of buildings, although only very slight traces of walling survive, in common with the medieval monastic plan it is here that we might expect to find the canons' chapter house. Their dormitory would probably have been located on the first floor.

The southern range of monastic buildings presumably lies under those converted farm structures outside the boundary wall. In almost all the known plans of Premonstratensian abbeys in Britain, the canons' refectory was situated on the first floor, and was arranged on an east–west axis over a vaulted basement or undercroft.

Although there are fragments of walls on the west side of the cloister, investigations in the 1930s failed to reveal any more substantial evidence for a range of buildings. At other houses of white canons, this block often provided cellarage, with a guest house or the abbot's lodging on the upper floor. But bearing in mind Talley's financial difficulties, it would not be surprising if the community failed to complete a fully conventual plan.

To the south-west of the principal remains there is a late medieval building of domestic character known as The King's Court (now a private house). It was almost certainly contained within the abbey precinct, and might have served as accommodation for a bailiff or steward connected with the monastic estate.

The remains of the three chapels in the south transept at Talley. Each chapel was covered with a stone barrel vault, with traces of that in the northern chapel (left) surviving against the adjacent presbytery wall.

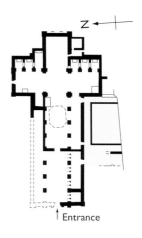

Entrance

A Tour of Strata Florida Abbey

Layout of the Abbey

Strata Florida Abbey is situated in an area of generally flat and lush meadowland bordering the banks of the river Teifi, which emerges hereabouts from its narrow upland valley. The site was chosen not least to take advantage of a spring of fresh water rising to the south-east, with the water brought to the monastic buildings through lead pipes. Drainage from the site, including the kitchens and latrines, was by way of a stone culvert, flushed by the small stream that can be seen running in front of the abbey across the valley towards the Teifi.

The gravel path that leads from the ticket office to the abbey church cuts across the medieval inner court, part of the much larger monastic precinct (p. 50). Access to this part of the inner court was probably controlled by a substantial gatehouse. Indeed, this may well be the structure which can be seen in the 1741 print of Strata Florida by Samuel and Nathaniel Buck, though it has since been demolished. The print shows windows above the level of the shallow central gate-arch, but we cannot be certain this is 'Penny Porth', a gate

with a chamber above mentioned in a sixteenth-century account.

At the far end of the path you will see the best preserved and most endearing feature of Strata Florida, the west doorway into the abbey church (see plan, inside back cover). To the left (north), behind what is a modern wall, lies the present churchyard. Through the doorway there is an unrestricted view eastwards along the entire length of the nave and presbytery towards the site of the high altar. To the right (south) of the nave lay the cloister, with the principal monastic buildings grouped around three sides.

Before proceeding, pause at the west doorway and observe some of the main features of the church plan.

The Abbey Church

The church lay at the heart of all communal monastic life. At Strata Florida, as elsewhere, it was by far the most important and the most used building within the entire abbey complex. In basic design, the church at Strata Florida followed the classic Cistercian 'Bernardine' plan (p. 25), which had become fully

The visitor centre is reached up steps and through a narrow doorway, but arrangements can be made with the custodian to enter the site through the exit gate, giving access to a firm, level path to the abbey ruins. The grounds are laid to grass.

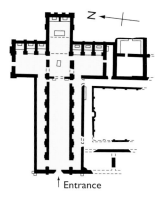

↑ Entrance

Below left: An engraving of Strata Florida by Samuel and Nathaniel Buck, 1741. The Stedman family had acquired the site by 1567, and it was they who built the later house to the south of the church. It may be the monastic inner gatehouse which features in the right foreground of the view (National Library of Wales).

Opposite: The best preserved and most endearing feature at Strata Florida is the west doorway into the abbey church. It is a truly striking composition, underlining the importance of both ritual and display. Regardless of whether it might embody elements of a Deheubarth 'court style', it was undoubtedly the work of a mason of considerable ingenuity.

developed by the mid-twelfth century. A cruciform or cross-shaped building, it was aligned east to west. Apart from the proportions and mass, the distinctive white monk features included the square-ended presbytery at the east, and the side-arm transepts with virtually square eastern chapels. At Strata Florida there were three chapels to each transept, when frequently — at both British and French abbeys — there were two. Overall, the building measured some 213 feet (65m) from east to west, by 117 feet (35.7m) across the transepts north to south.

As with Cistercian churches in general, Strata Florida was built to serve two almost entirely separate communities: the lay brothers (*conversi*) who used the nave or western half; and the choir monks, who followed a much stricter regime, and whose lives were regulated around long hours spent in their choir stalls towards the east end of the building.

A reconstruction of the west front of the abbey church at Strata Florida as it may have appeared around 1250. More speculatively, the scene depicts a stage during the monks' procession on Palm Sunday. Having passed through the cloister walks, blessing the various buildings, the community is shown about to return into the church through the west doorway (Illustration by Terry Ball, 2007).

The West Front

The late twelfth-century west doorway, or portal, is a truly striking composition betraying a mason of remarkable ingenuity. It is without close parallel, not just in Wales but among Cistercian architecture anywhere in the British Isles. A spiral motif around the hood mould of doorways can, for example, be seen at Fountains Abbey in Yorkshire, and the banded effect across the columns appears at Margam Abbey. But it is the whole composition that is unique at Strata Florida. There were originally six orders of continuous roll mouldings, all devoid of capitals, but divided by thirteen cross-bands, each of which terminates with a scroll or spiral ornament. The bands perhaps bear a certain resemblance to croziers, a common motif on Cistercian tomb slabs. The inner order of the doorway was lost during nineteenth-century repairs, which sought to prevent the arch from falling.

Above the doorway, there were almost certainly three tall, pointed lancet windows, and there was possibly a circular opening, or oculus, higher up into the pointed gable. To the north and south, each of the side aisles at this end of the nave was lit with a single lancet, with that in the south aisle now the only window in the entire abbey that remains intact. The vertical scar between the doorway and this window represents one of the stepped buttresses that can be seen in the Buck engraving of Strata Florida.

The west doorway itself was not intended for regular use by the community. Its importance lay in display, and in ritual and ceremony. It would, for instance, have provided a magnificent climax to a carefully controlled approach through the abbey precinct. The monks themselves used this grand entrance during important processions, such as on Palm Sunday. They would have re-entered the church this way after all the abbey buildings had been blessed. They then processed along the nave and entered the choir for High Mass.

The Nave

You should now move through the west doorway and enter the nave, that part of the church initially reserved for the lay brothers. They would have assembled for worship in their wooden choir stalls, which were arranged facing inwards along the length of the central area. In all, the nave extended to seven bays, with a bay defined as the space between

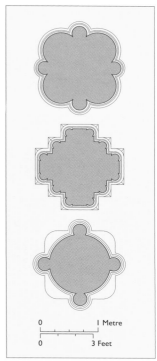

each pair of piers running along the length of the building. Apart from the first bay, the central part of the nave was screened off from the north and south aisles by continuous partition walls, originally standing up to 5 feet (1.5m) high. The aisles themselves would have served essentially as passages. Screen walls between piers were more common than can now be demonstrated, and are known to have existed for instance at the abbeys of Byland and Fountains in Yorkshire, at Tintern, and at Baltinglass and Jerpoint in Ireland. If stone was not used, then Cistercian naves must have been almost habitually separated from their aisles by wooden screens.

Strata Florida is of particular interest in that the piers stood on top of the screen walls (see reconstructions, pp. 42–43). Having passed through the west doorway, immediately to the right is the lower section of a respond, or half-pier, representing the west end of the south arcade. Elsewhere along the nave, a thickening in the outer face of the screen walls indicates the positions of the remaining piers. Overall, these nave piers — which were of at least three different designs — together with the arches of the arcades above, must have presented a rather

Above: Drawings to show the three designs of nave arcade piers at Strata Florida (Stuart Harrison).

Above left: The nave arcade piers at Strata Florida stood on solid partition walls. Standing up to 5 feet (1.5m) high, the walls screened off the central area of the nave from aisles to the north and south. As this view looking south-east shows, the screen walls survive as foundations. The projecting dressed-stone plinths mark the positions of the piers.

Left: A Cistercian lay brother, depicted in a manuscript of about 1269–70. Over his shoulder he carries what may be a sack of wool, or perhaps a roll of cloth (British Library, Additional Ms. 48978, f. 41v).

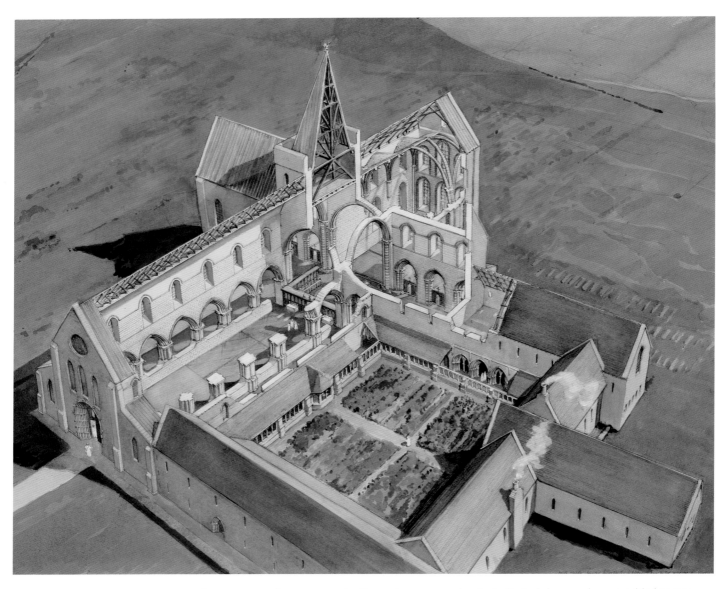

A reconstruction of Strata Florida to suggest its appearance towards the end of the fifteenth century. The cutaway of the church shows the form of the nave piers, as well as the stone vault within the presbytery. The cloister court to the south is depicted as a garden. The form of the monastic buildings, especially on the south and west sides, is necessarily conjectural (Illustration by Terry Ball, 1998; with amendments, 2007).

squat appearance when compared with most Cistercian churches. However, the arrangement was not altogether without reason, since the lay brothers' choir stalls would have backed on to the walls and masked the lower sections.

Without records, we cannot be sure how many lay brothers sat in the Strata Florida stalls, and the loss of much of the west range (p. 55) makes it difficult to estimate the provision made for their accommodation. In this context, you should note the narrow doorway leading to a small staircase in the far south-west corner of the church. The staircase,

despite its limited size, may have provided access from the lay brothers' dormitory down to the nave for services at night.

In the twelfth and thirteenth centuries, men such as these — anxious to give their labour to the service of God — flocked to the gates of Cistercian abbeys all over Europe. Despite problems of discipline (p. 13), it is estimated the *conversi* outnumbered the choir monks at this time by at least a factor of two to one. They took religious vows and wore the habit, but they were illiterate men and were required by their specific rule book to remain so. They took part in fewer services, mainly the night offices, spending much of the day in the fields where they would recite a few simple prayers learned by heart.

Before leaving the lay brothers' area of the church, we should consider the upper walls of the nave, where a row of clerestory windows doubtless ran along the top of the arcades, giving a simple two-storey elevation typical of the early Cistercians. The wall faces may have been 'articulated' — that is given greater architectural emphasis — with shafts running up between the windows, adding greater rhythm to the bay divisions, but we cannot be certain of the details.

From the evidence that survives, it seems that neither the central area of the nave nor the aisles were ever vaulted in stone. Throughout the Middle Ages, the roofs were probably supported on wooden trusses, though the underside of these could have been boarded to represent vaulting. As to the floors, we know from the excavations of the 1880s that a substantial area in the eastern half of the nave was eventually covered with a tile pavement. In this pavement, four large areas of diagonally set tiles were divided by a cross, picked out in two bands of the same tiles. The tiles themselves, of which a small patch survives not far from the entrance to the monks' choir, date from about 1250–1300, though they may have been reset. The aisles, meanwhile, were perhaps paved in plain slabs. Doorways at either end of the south aisle, which are now robbed of their jambs, communicated with the east and west walks of the cloister (see ground plan inside back cover).

The nave was separated from the monks' choir by a screen wall known as a pulpitum. The stone footings of this screen survive. Set against the nave side were two altars, the bases of which can still be seen. The nineteenth-century excavations revealed burials in front of these altars.

Far left: A conjectural reconstruction of the two-storey nave elevation at Strata Florida (Stuart Harrison).

The nave at Strata Florida was separated from the monks' choir by a screen known as the pulpitum. Although incomplete, stone foundations representing this screen survive, with the bases of two altars facing west (left) towards the nave.

The east end of the church at Strata Florida with the monks' choir in the foreground. Beyond the remains of the massive eastern crossing piers is the presbytery, where a stone plinth marks the position of the high altar. The south transept is to the right.

The Monks' Choir

At the centre of the church, four great pointed arches formed the 'crossing', the point between the nave and presbytery, and between the north and south transepts. All that remain are the bases of the substantial piers which supported these arches. Above this central area rose the squat tower or belfry in which a single bell was hung in 1255 (p. 28). As we have seen, the crossing was separated from the nave by the pulpitum screen, and further walls to the north and south cut off the transepts. This enclosed area was reserved exclusively for the monks. Their stalls, which were probably quite elaborate timber constructions by the end of the Middle Ages, backed on to the screen walls on all three sides.

The observance of what St Benedict called the *opus Dei* (the work of God) provided the basic framework in the monks' day. From the *Rule of St Benedict*, they followed the example of the Old Testament psalmist, singing the praises of God seven times a day, and at night rising to confess him. In all, this meant eight long services or divine offices in the choir. Everything else had to be fitted around the essential routine, day in, day out. At about 2.00 to 3.00 a.m. the monks were stirred from sleep by the

bell, assembling in the choir to sing the office of Nocturns (later called Matins). With intervals for the chapter meeting (p. 53), work and dinner, they continued through to the last service of Compline, which took place sometime around 6.00 to 8.00 p.m. depending on the time of year.

In the original liturgical arrangements, as completed in the very early years of the thirteenth century, the choir may have been enclosed by timber screens. At the east (or presbytery) end of the monks' stalls were the upper choir entrances. The cut in the base of the north-east crossing pier may have been made to accommodate the northern doorway. During this same early phase, it is very likely that the stalls themselves extended further westward, that is into the first bay of the nave. Indeed, the lower parts of the western crossing piers were left perfectly flat so as to accommodate the backs of the stalls. The insertion of the surviving stone walls probably formed part of a liturgical reordering of the choir, and can probably be attributed to rebuilding after the fire of 1284/86, and the further destruction in 1294–95. The tile pavement laid across this area in the earlier fourteenth century must have been particularly attractive. Above, the north and south arches of the crossing added to the decorative effect,

Opposite: A manuscript illustration of 1268 depicting two scenes from the east end of an abbey church, from the Cistercian abbey at Zwettl in Austria. In the lower register, seven monks grouped around a lectern in the choir sing loud and clear. In the upper register, a priest-monk stands at the high altar at the elevation of the Host. Behind him a kneeling monk is shown ringing a bell (Stiftsbibliothek Zwettl, Ms 400, f. 1v).

constructed as they were in alternate bands of purple Caerbwdy stone and cream limestone.

Near the centre of the floor in the choir there is a stone-lined basin, with steps at either end. It was discovered during clearance operations after the site was taken into State care, sometime between 1935 and 1949. There have been suggestions that it was used in a rite known as the *mandatum*, where on the Thursday of Holy Week the abbot washed the feet of twelve brothers: four monks, four novices, and four lay brothers. Although the basin is not regularly aligned, and despite the fact the prescribed place for the *mandatum* ceremony was in the cloister, there is much to commend such a ritual interpretation to this intriguing feature. A rather more mundane view is that it was constructed in connection with a drain laid out across the site. The upper edges were rebated to receive a cover or enclosing slab, but we cannot be sure how this was reflected in the tile pavement.

The Presbytery

The area to the east of the choir is known as the presbytery. This was the site of the high altar at which the daily community Mass was celebrated. The initial design of this part of the church may well

Strata Florida: The Decoration in the Church

A detail of leaf decoration on a fragment of carved stonework from Strata Florida (David Robinson).

This carved-stone head of a Cistercian monk was found during the excavations of Strata Florida in 1887–90. It probably dates from the thirteenth century.

From the ruins that survive today, it is perhaps difficult to picture the rich decorative appearance we would have encountered in the church at Strata Florida during the Middle Ages. To begin with, apart from a variety in the design of the great piers and arches of the arcades, the capitals were carved in rich foliate patterns. The contrasts and richness were further highlighted by the use of different coloured stonework, with alternating bands of pale cream limestone from the Bristol Channel area, and deep purple Caerbwdy stone from quarries near St Davids. The use of alternating bands of coloured stone was a technique extending back at least to the early twelfth century in the west and south-west of England, and can still be seen to glorious effect in, for example, St Davids Cathedral.

The rubble core of the walls was plastered, probably both inside and out. The inner walls were then decorated with various painted motifs and geometric designs, including a diaper pattern. There were also floral themes, and some indication of the richness still survives on the plaster in the south transept chapels. Following the fire of the 1280s, the walls were subsequently whitewashed, a covering that hid scorch marks on both stone and earlier plaster.

We know, too, from fragments recovered in the excavations of the 1880s, that at least some of the windows were filled with coloured glass. In turn, the overall appearance would have been complemented in the later Middle Ages by the sheen from the glazed and slip-coated tiles at the east end of the church.

There was also much more wood than we may imagine throughout the church. The roofs of the nave and its aisles were probably always of wood, and may have been boarded and painted. By the fifteenth century, some of the carved woodwork was of particularly high quality. Elaborate screens, for instance, drew the attention of the bards who sang the praises of the abbots at this time.

Nor should we forget the various tombs and memorials scattered throughout the church, which would have added to the full decorative effect.

The east end of the presbytery at Strata Florida. The stone foundations of two altars, separated by a dividing wall, indicate a pair of small chapels against the gable wall.

have born a strong resemblance to Burgundian Cistercian prototypes; it was perhaps intended to carry a stone barrel vault. However, a scheme which involved a modest eastwards extension, together with the insertion of a more elaborate rib vault, was soon in hand. On the external faces of the presbytery, buttresses and a low plinth at the foot of the walls mark the extension.

The two steps up from the choir (now almost entirely grassed over) belong to modifications of the early fourteenth century, when the entire east end of the church was covered with slip-coated and glazed tiles. Part way along the presbytery, another step — also grass covered — marks the position of the sanctuary as further reorganized apparently towards the end of the Middle Ages. At this time, the high altar was moved close to the edge of the sanctuary step, where the consolidated base now marks its approximate position. Two small chapels with subsidiary altars may have been set up against the east wall, and this is certainly the arrangement as

determined during consolidation works after 1931. At a later point (possibly even after the suppression), the whole of the sanctuary area was paved in a chequer pattern of red and black tiles, covering the level of the fourteenth-century pavement.

Fragments found during the excavations of the 1880s suggest there was a sedilia and a piscina in the recess in the south wall. The former would have provided seating for the monks celebrating Mass, and the latter was a small sink for washing the sacred vessels used in the service.

In the two eastern corners are the columns that rose to support the springers of the presbytery vault. The later raised flooring conceals the bases, but they are known from excavation to be of an early type. They were presumably moved here when the presbytery was extended. The stone rib vault, which protected this part of the church from the fire of 1284/86 (p. 29), was introduced as part of the extended presbytery at the very end of the twelfth century. The vault was arranged in three bays, in which

In each of the eastern corners of the presbytery at Strata Florida there are traces of a circular column. These columns rose all the way to the springing of the stone vault. The column bases were buried when the floor level was raised in the later Middle Ages.

The Strata Florida Precinct

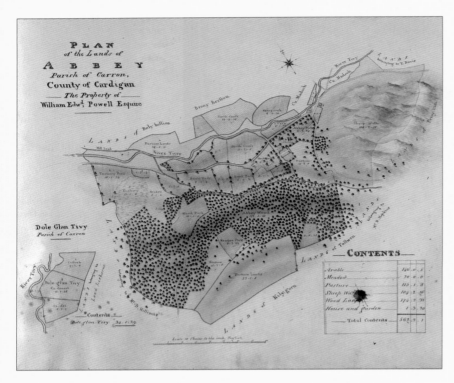

A plan of 1819 showing 'the Lands of the Abbey', then the property of William Edward Powell. The Powell holdings at Strata Florida still represented the former monastic precinct and the core of the Cistercian home estate. The northern side of the precinct was bounded by the river Teifi, and the southern side by the edge of Abbey Wood seen here (National Library of Wales, vol. 45, p. 59).

Although the church and principal claustral buildings were at the heart of all Cistercian abbeys, they covered but a small percentage of the total ground area. The monastic precinct as a whole tended to be a very much larger entity, and in this Strata Florida was no exception. Indeed, in a Welsh context, the bounds of the full complex at Strata Florida appear to have been exceptionally large.

The northern and southern sides of the precinct were probably determined by the river Teifi and its tributary, the Glasffrwd, both of which may have been partially engineered into artificial channels. There are the remains of a large masonry wall following a contour on the hillside to the east of the church and cloister. Entrance through this great enclosure was controlled by several gatehouses, at least one of which featured an attendant porter's lodge. In the fifteenth century, for example, the poet Guto'r Glyn wrote of the food and charity offered to both rich and poor at Strata Florida's southern gate.

Inside the western half of the precinct boundary, a wide cross section of visitors, monastic officials, and servants would be found in the outer court, a busy and bustling area doubtless housing both agricultural and industrial buildings essential to the exploitation of the abbey's estates. The field to the immediate west of the ticket office (adjacent to the modern car park) was known in the sixteenth century as the 'Cowart Green' (Convent Green).

Entrance to the inner court was probably controlled by another gatehouse, perhaps represented by a building seen in the Buck print of 1741 (p. 39). Access to the inner court would have been far more limited, and probably restricted to men. Within its vicinity we might have expected to find buildings such as a bakehouse, a brewhouse and guest accommodation. Even by the end of the twelfth century, when many of the subsidiary abbey buildings were doubtless still of timber construction, there is a suggestion that guests generally expected a level of hospitality according to their status. About 1200, Gerald of Wales complained bitterly of his accommodation at Strata Florida when he was 'harboured in the public hall among the common guests and the noise of the people'.

Long before the suppression, a chapel had been built within the monastery for lay people, who were otherwise many miles from a parish church. This may survive in part as the parish church to the north of the abbey ruins.

The Strata Florida precinct as a whole is the subject of a wide-ranging new archaeological and landscape study. Important results have already emerged, including the discovery of a large mill with its leat system, a possible gatehouse, and the site of the monks' infirmary. In the surrounding area, topographical elements relating to the community's wider exploitation of natural resources are beginning to be unpicked. Among other discoveries, the research may have led to the identification of a tile-working site. In all, as the work progresses, it will provide us with a much clearer understanding of the extensive Cistercian landscape surrounding the core buildings at Strata Florida.

The Cloister
and Monastic Buildings

The monastic buildings — those structures where the community slept, where meals were prepared and eaten, where business was conducted and where the brothers took some relaxation — were situated to the south of the abbey church. They were grouped around three sides of an open square or court known as the cloister. The central square itself was occasionally left grassed, though more commonly it was laid out as a garden, perhaps for culinary and medicinal herbs.

Two doorways in the south aisle of the nave (p. 43) linked the church with the cloister. That towards the east end was once an elaborate entrance,

now totally robbed of its dressed stonework, and was the doorway through which the choir monks passed into the church for services during the day. To the west, the second doorway was probably used initially by the lay brothers to enter the nave.

The greater part of the cloister can still be seen, though the southern end lies buried beneath the confines of the late seventeenth-century Stedman house (Great Abbey Farm). We must imagine the central court surrounded on all four sides by walkways, or alleys, each covered by a lean-to roof. In the earlier Middle Ages, the sides facing the court would have featured open rhythmic arcading, probably supported on twin stone columns. But in the fifteenth century both the arcades, and presumably the roofs, were entirely rebuilt. As completed, groups of five pointed windows were carried on dwarf walls, with each group flanked by

Below: An aerial view of Strata Florida from the south-west. In the foreground, the cloister and its surrounding buildings have only been partially investigated. Great Abbey Farm, set at right angles to the cloister, lies over the site of the monks' refectory (Skyscan Balloon Photography, for Cadw).

The projection in the wall of the north cloister alley at Strata Florida provided a bay in which to place a lectern. During the evening ceremony known as Collation, one of the monks would have stood here to read to his brothers.

projecting buttresses (see reconstruction drawing, p. 54). Altogether, this made for far more comfortable surroundings, particularly during the winter months.

On the north side, the alley against the church was the recognized place for private study. Near the middle of this alley, the later arcade was angled out towards the court. This projecting bay provided an alcove, and it was here that one of the monks stood at a lectern to read to his brothers during the evening ceremony known as Collation. The name of the ceremony was taken from the *Collationes* of St John Cassian (d. 435), one of the books recommended for reading. The monks sat and listened on a stone bench set against the wall of the church. Following this reading, they all entered the church for the last service of the day, Compline.

On the east side of the cloister, a long two-storey range of buildings ran southwards projecting from the line of the south transept. In the plan common to Cistercian abbeys, the monks' dormitory occupied the entire upper floor of this range. Somewhere along its outer length, depending on the location and arrangements of the main drainage system, there was a latrine block also reserved for the monks.

The Book Store and Sacristy

On the ground floor, the space immediately beside the south transept now looks as though it was a single chamber. For at least some part of the abbey's history, however, it was divided into two rooms. The position of the dividing wall is known from the excavations of the 1880s.

The smaller room, with a doorway from the cloister, was the *armarium* or the abbey's book store. The *Rule of St Benedict* stressed the importance of divine reading (*lectio divina*) in the life of a monk, and time was set aside during the Cistercian day for this purpose. Each monk may have collected a volume from the book store, taking it to the north walk of the cloister where the best sunlight would be found. We should remember, too, that the monks at Strata Florida wrote and kept the manuscript that was the source of *Brut y Tywysogyon* (*Chronicle of the Princes*), and they are also likely to have been involved in copying works of Welsh literature. Such volumes, written and read in the cloister, were stored in the *armarium*.

The larger room to the east, with a doorway directly into the church, served as the sacristy. It was under the charge of one of the senior monks, the sacristan, and was the place where the vestments and liturgical vessels used in the services were stored in safety. There is the base of a lancet window in the east wall, and the pit nearby represents part of the burial vault for the tomb in the south transept chapel.

The Chapter House

Adjoining the south wall of the sacristy and book store was the chapter house, once a large and imposing room of great importance. The monks gathered here each morning, sitting on benching around the outer walls, whilst the abbot presided over the chapter meeting. A lesson was read, along with a chapter from the *Rule of St Benedict* (hence the name of the room), and occasionally the abbot delivered a sermon. It was here, too, that the brothers confessed their faults, or were accused by others, and were assigned penances. The chapter house was also the place where business and administrative matters of concern to the community would be discussed.

The structural history of the Strata Florida chapter house appears to have been quite complex, and it would require thorough archaeological excavation to elucidate matters more fully. Nevertheless, we might expect that the foundations were laid out with the church in the late twelfth century, and it is feasible that the building was initially contained within the basic width of the east range. If so, its scale is likely to have equated to the current

The narrow bay adjacent to the south transept at Strata Florida was originally divided into two rooms. In the foreground, facing the cloister, was the book store. The sacristy was positioned to the rear, with a door giving access directly into the church.

This manuscript illustration of Bernard of Clairvaux, with two monks reading at his feet, reminds us of the importance of books in Cistercian life. The north walk of the cloister was the recognized place for private study (Bodleian Library, Oxford, Ms. Laud Misc. 385, f. 41v).

Below: The chapter house at Strata Florida, as completed in the thirteenth century, was a large and imposing room of great importance to the community. It was also the burial place of many descendants of the Lord Rhys (David Robinson).

A reconstruction of the chapter house façade and the fifteenth-century cloister arcades at Strata Florida, based on loose stone fragments recovered from the site. The nave of the abbey church is to the left, the south transept at the centre, and the monks' dormitory over the chapter house to the right (Illustration by Terry Ball, from original details by Stuart Harrison, 1998).

grass-covered area. Next, we can deduce from stone fragments recovered during the investigations of the 1880s that the entrance façade was remodelled in the early thirteenth century, perhaps in the 1220s. It is possible, therefore, that the eastwards extension of the chapter house (now the current gravel-covered area) also dates from this time. In the newly completed entrance façade, both the jambs and the arch-head of the central doorway were heavily moulded. The capitals featured bulbous stiff-leaf

foliage. There was a further moulded archway to either side of the doorway, with the whole arrangement fairly typical of Cistercian abbeys. Parts of the present wall along the line of the entrance are likely to be post-monastic.

Within the chapter house, there are traces of the stone benches on which the monks sat along the side walls. And, although we cannot be certain, it would have been unusual if this important chamber were not covered with a stone vault. In many

monasteries, it was customary to bury the abbots in the chapter house. This may have been true in part at Strata Florida, but here the room was certainly used very extensively for the burial of other important personages. In the thirteenth century, it became a virtual burial vault for the Deheubarth dynasty of princes, the descendants of the Lord Rhys.

At a later date, perhaps following the community's troubles at the end of the thirteenth century, the chapter house was reduced in size. A cross wall — which hitherto may have served as the division between an outer vestibule and the chapter house proper — was fully blocked. The projecting east end must have been removed, and the area was given over to burial with graves cut through the earlier foundations. Parts of the blocking have been unpicked, revealing the base of a window in the northern half of the wall, and you will see a moulded base in the gap near the centre.

The original floor level in the chapter house is indicated by the replica grave slab near the north wall (the original is in the ticket office). When opened in the 1880s, this grave was found to contain a mass of human bones, including at least twelve skulls. There is a possibility that burials from the east projection were grouped here when the room was reduced in size.

The West Range

Over on the opposite side of the cloister there are slight traces of the west range, a building which has never been cleared or excavated. Essentially, it was another two-storey block running southwards from the church, and in the thirteenth century it would have served to accommodate the abbey's many lay brothers.

In the normal Cistercian arrangement, the ground floor of the west range was divided into a number of compartments. One of the principal spaces was occupied as the lay brothers' refectory, and another large area is likely to have been used for cellarage. The west range was also the location of the outer parlour. It was here that the abbey cellarer (who usually had an office in the west range) met and conversed with tradesmen and other visitors on matters of estate business and provisions for the community. The entire upper floor of the west range would have served as the lay brothers' dormitory.

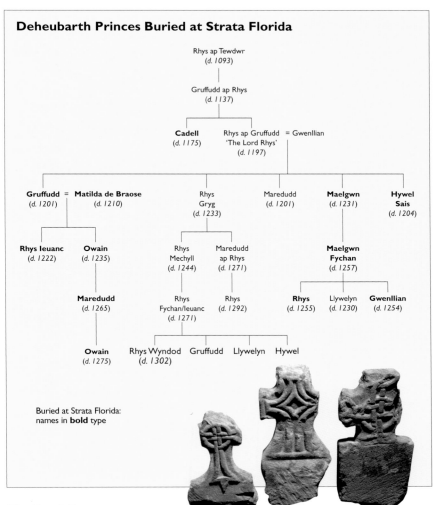

Deheubarth Princes Buried at Strata Florida

Buried at Strata Florida: names in **bold** type

An important series of grave-markers was discovered at Strata Florida during the excavations of the late 1880s. Found outside the church, in the angle between the south transept and the presbytery, they were presumably erected to commemorate important patrons of the abbey (National Museum of Wales).

The South Range

The south range lies buried behind the modern boundary wall which cuts off this side of the cloister. Again, in the standard Cistercian plan, this range included three principal chambers. On the east side, there was generally a warming house, the place where a fire was lit during the winter months to provide some comfort for the monks during their time spent in the cloister. On the west side was the abbey kitchen, located in a position where it might serve both the refectories of the lay brothers and the choir monks.

The monks' refectory was itself located in the central position. In the standard Cistercian plan, that is from the later twelfth century onwards, it was usually a substantial rectangular chamber set at right angles to the cloister. The doorway from the cloister

The figure of Christ from a crucifix dating from the first half of the thirteenth century, found at Strata Florida. The piece is just under 5 inches (121mm) high (National Museum of Wales).

was often flanked by a pair of lavers, lead-lined stone basins in which the monks washed before going into meals. The position of the Stedman house (Great Abbey Farm) in this area suggests this later building occupies a part of the site, and perhaps even some of the structure, of the medieval refectory.

Finally, outside the three main ranges of the cloister, we might expect to find some trace of other buildings lying under the surrounding turf. The infirmary, for example, said to be ruinous by the suppression (p. 30), seems to have been located in the field to the south-east where there are substantial earthworks marking the remains of structures. It would not be unusual to find the abbot's private block of accommodation in the same general area.

Further Reading

Acknowledgements
As in earlier editions of this guide, the principal author and Cadw would like to acknowledge the assistance provided by Mr W. T. Ball, Mr C. J. Bond, the late Professor Sir Rees Davies, the late Mr T. A. James, Mr C. Jones-Jenkins, Dr R. K. Morris, Mr R. F. Suggett, and the Reverend Dr D. H. Williams. The Strata Florida sections in this new edition again benefit from the very significant contribution made by Mr S. A. Harrison; and Professor David Austin has kindly shared his initial views on the abbey's precinct and the wider Cistercian landscape.

Strata Florida Abbey
David Austin, 'Strata Florida and its Landscape', *Archaeologia Cambrensis* **153** (2004), 192–201.

E. G. Bowen, 'The Monastic Economy of the Cistercians at Strata Florida', *Ceredigion* **I** (1950–51), 34–37.

T. Jones Pierce, 'Strata Florida Abbey', *Ceredigion* **I** (1950–51), 18–33.

C. A. R. Radford, *Strata Florida Abbey* (HMSO, London 1949).

J. Beverley Smith and W. G. Thomas, *Abaty Ystrad Fflur* (HMSO, London 1977).

Stephen W. Williams, *The Cistercian Abbey of Strata Florida* (London 1889).

Stephen W. Williams, 'Strata Florida Abbey: Report on Further Excavations, June 1890', *Archaeologia Cambrensis*, 5th series, **7** (1890), 253–56.

Talley Abbey
B. H. St J. O'Neil, 'Talley Abbey, Carmarthenshire', *Archaeologia Cambrensis* **96** (1941), 69–91.

Edward Owen, 'A Contribution to the History of the Præmonstratensian Abbey of Talley', *Archaeologia Cambrensis*, 5th series, **10** (1893), 29–47, 120–28, 226–37, 309–25; **11** (1894), 34–50, 92–107, 196–213.

Melville Richards, 'The Carmarthenshire Possessions of Talyllychau', in Tudor Barnes and Nigel Yates (editors), *Carmarthenshire Studies* (Carmarthen 1974), 110–21.

Dylan Roberts and Richard Suggett, 'A Late-Medieval Monastic Hall-House Rediscovered: The King's Court, Talyllychau', *Carmarthenshire Antiquary* **35** (1999), 5–11.

J. Beverley Smith and B. H. St J. O'Neil, *Talley Abbey* (HMSO, London 1967).

Stephen W. Williams, 'Excavations at Talley Abbey', *Archaeologia Cambrensis*, 5th series, **14** (1897), 229–47.

General Historical and Monastic Background
James Bond, 'The Premonstratensian Order: A Preliminary Survey of its Growth and Distribution in Medieval Europe', in Martin Carver (editor), *In Search of Cult* (Woodbridge 1993), 153–85.

Janet Burton, *Monastic and Religious Orders in Britain 1000–1300* (Cambridge 1994).

A. W. Clapham, 'The Architecture of the Premonstratensians, with Special Reference to their Buildings in England', *Archaeologia* **73** (1922–23), 117–46.

H. M. Colvin, *The White Canons in England* (Oxford 1951).

F. G. Cowley, *The Monastic Order in South Wales, 1066–1349* (Cardiff 1977).

R. R. Davies, *Conquest, Coexistence, and Change: Wales 1063–1415* (Oxford 1987); reprinted in paperback as, *The Age of Conquest: Wales 1063–1415* (Oxford 1991).

J. Patrick Greene, *Medieval Monasteries* (Leicester 1992).

Henrietta Leyser, *Hermits and the New Monasticism: A Study of Religious Communities in Western Europe 1000–1150* (London 1984).

Huw Pryce, 'Yr Eglwys yn Oes yr Arglwydd Rhys', in Nerys Anne Jones and Huw Pryce (editors), *Yr Arglwydd Rhys* (Cardiff 1996), 145–77.

David Robinson (editor), *The Cistercian Abbeys of Britain: Far From the Concourse of Men* (London 1998); reprinted in paperback (London 2002).

David M. Robinson, *The Cistercians in Wales: Architecture and Archaeology 1130–1540* (London 2006).

David H. Williams, *The Welsh Cistercians*, new edition (Leominster 2001).

David H. Williams, *The Cistercians in the Early Middle Ages* (Leominster 1998).

Glanmor Williams, *The Welsh Church from Conquest to Reformation*, 2nd edition (Cardiff 1976).

A late twelfth-century capital, with trumpet scallop and leaf decoration, from the south transept of Strata Florida.